Solid 6

The Common Man's Guide to Dating in the Romantic Dark Age

A. R. Valancy

*For the guys who, upon first shaking
a chick's hand, hear wedding bells*

Contents

Part One

Intro

What This Book is . . .

What I'm presenting here is a means with which you can begin to build for yourself the strongest and surely, the most realistic foundation on which to build your romantic goals. To elaborate, utilizing a homebuilding metaphor, this book is about selecting the best land on which to construct our "house", and subsequently starting that construction on the finest, sturdiest quality *foundation* that we can. We'll be doing that through education and experience. A process by which this book acts as merely as a resource to help you get rolling, to be used alongside whatever additional tools that you have in your assortment.

I've endeavored to format *Solid 6* in such a manner as to be a brisk page-turner, a resource that the reader can digest as ready-made, easily deriving benefit from it, even off of the first read. The anticipated arduousness of the full brunt of the quest aside, some preliminary results can indeed be expected to be gleaned, without requiring a boot-camp of introspection, transitional phasing in personality/mannerisms, or physique transformation (not to start, anyway).

Concepts over a wide berth will be glossed over and inter-connected, their major tenets highlighted. Topics will be referenced, as they find pertinence within the scope of this book, but without an exhaustive study of any one particular phenomenon or idea. To be sure, the mention of such brings us to the summarization of what *Solid 6* is not.

What This Book is Not . . .

As previously noted, this book is not meant to be a definitive source for wildly-encompassing material such as intergender dynamics, principles in Game, hypergamy, and such. Other authors have all ready dedicated their effort in publishing whole volumes on these topics, and to a far greater degree of thoroughness that I could ever dare to endeavor upon. Such books shall be referenced here, where appropriate, as well as formally listed later. Again, this book is merely an assemblage of a wide spectrum of ideas and schools of thought, painted with a wide brush, so that the multitude of colors can be distinguished.

In addition, I'll have to admit, that this is not a guide to maintaining a relationship, nor is it marriage counseling. As stated above, authors specializing in such have their books available, and so, *Solid 6* is designed to be a *companion piece* to such. My specialization, and subsequently, the bulk of my professed experience deals with the base, rudimentary stages for a man to grapple with in *starting* his expedition into dating in the present age, or perhaps re-starting it. This is a *beginning* guide. Again, here we're gonna survey the land and set that foundation. The building of the house, I'll leave for you to endeavor upon, utilizing a wealth of additional resource materials. I'll act as the introductory valet that greets you at the gate of this grand manor, leading you up the main path and to the front door.

Lastly, this is not a sex manual (yeah, so go ahead and shelve the fucker). We're not gonna get into techniques and mannerisms with which you can better please a woman in that regard. Heh, let's worry about *getting* you a goddamn woman in the first place – and one who'll have receptively open legs for you, as opposed to friend-zoning you, ghosting you, or any of that stupid shit. Now, averting that kind of scenario to as minimal of a prevalence as possible . . . *that* is what this book is all about.

Target Audience

In actuality, this book may very well appeal to a commanding swath of the male demographic. The focal group, really though, would be the majority of dudes somewhere amidst the vast realm of "average" on the spectrum, and perhaps even lower than that. My tendency to think in extremes does, occasionally domineer my philosophy, and nay, when the topic of dating today, in the "smartphone" era, is the focus of the discussion, conclusions made in extremes tend to achieve an unfortunate prominence.

To laser-in on an example pertinent to this volume, you'll find a lot of yap in the literature about how "it's over" for average guys, with the top 20% monopolizing 80% of chicks. Well hell, you could even figure the bottom *95%* of dudes today might as well go fuck themselves. Extremist conclusion? Well, let's hope so. The coaching and strategy found here is going to be all about building the best you, and getting you out in the field and giving it a shot . . . and to be sensibly realistic about your expectations and goals.

As the very title implies, though admittedly in a satirical sense, *Solid 6* is about formulating a reasonable, realistic standard in dating achievement. As we'll discuss later, the title, in its nudging at the reader as to what we know of as a rather mediocre rating on the "1-10" scale, men today have become conditioned to see as this as some far-reaching goal.

Hey, if some chode who picks up this book, whips himself into sufficient shape to land himself a gal who's a "6", then I've fulfilled my job rather admirably. And he'll be free to reach for even farther-flung stars. On top of that, I won't be one to shame him if he opts to try dating a chick who's a single mother, or is past 25, or is two fuckin' hours older than him, or happens to be his co-worker (just be cognizant of the unique hazards of such).

In that spirit, I'll refrain from the kind of high-handed preaching found in many other avenues, bombarding the reader with admonishment to "just be confident and get out there, and you can have a different girl in your bed every night", or hammer into the all ready self-doubting mind of some 35-year-old twig-boy on how his ass should be hitting up the 8s, 9s, and 10s, and college girls and shit. C'mon, admirable ambitions, to be certain, but hardly realistic. Hey, fuck, we'll *try* for that level – but I sure as shit won't be one to *promise* it to you.

Online forums of the like are generously peppered with lofty keyboard-jockeying from dudes supposedly maintaining harems of sorts, smoothly regaling exploits of wrangling multiple women, "spinning plates", topped off with a "main girl". Reading this shit, you're likely to wonder as to just what planet these guys are comin' from, and how it's all gotta be some epic bullshit, or you just might even be lulled into assessing these notions as somethin' to shoot for yourself.

Let's start by just getting out of bed, and planting our feet down to fuckin' stand before we endeavor to even take a step. I'll state now, that what I *can* guarantee for you is some, measurable degree of results. Might not prove to be the most stellar degree of product you anticipated (at least early on), but you'll be better off than you were before.

This book is an arena for those guys that are really having a problem, and need to get educated in how things are, and how things work. I do feel that even seasoned veterans may find an insight or two here. But really, a fella of an advanced order would be far better suited to delve into the much high-caliber volumes.

Men who are bogged down by certain social ineptitudes, or perhaps men who are really quite solid, but are lacking in merely a few minute, but critical areas, can find a good start to get rolling here.

Solid 6 is geared for the guy whose dating experience is either non-existent or not sufficiently extensive to yield him the desired success. An array of tools, stratagem and philosophy will be provided here, with which the reader can use for the building of that very experience necessary toward achieving his objectives. You will learn not only how to get dates in an acceptably short segment of time, but also, the most practical and rational attitudes that you as a man should have toward women, dating, romantic conquest, and toward yourself.

This book offers concise perspectives on the current dating climate, as well as insight as to its navigation. All of this shall be presented in shades that I hope will be unique, as opposed to being rhetoric that merely overlaps what a bunch of other guys are all ready saying.

Commentary On the Current Dating Market

It's a true rock-solid golden age for women. An era without parallel in the history of the universe. Not just in dating, but cutting a swath through a multitude of regards. Now, I'll forego any hefty discussion along the lines of how today's societal constructs and institutions, marital court systems etc., favor the advancement of women, as truly masterful texts have thusly been penned on such, as shall be referenced in the final part. However, the scope of this manual will, indeed, make highlights regarding the insidious breadth of advantage women now hold within the realm of dating. Bring your best umbrella, 'cause it's gonna be a shitstorm.

Primarily due to the advent of technologies such as the smartphone and social media, among many other factors, women have been enabled to garner an audience of attention wildly outpacing the radius possible at any previous time period in history. The interconnectivity potential is simply without precedence.

Even a genuinely lame chick can now toss up a bullshit album of herself and her generic exploits across a multitude of social media platforms, and consequently amass a veritable army of (mostly male) admirers, thus inflating her ego and sense of value to staggeringly ridiculous levels. 2 is the new 6, 5 is the new 9, and 7 is the new *12*.

How all of these factors leech into the world of dating and relationships is that once a woman is cognizant of this literally, global network of attention and potential suitors, she can be so prone as to "second-guess" her decision as to if who she's paired up with – or considering to be so – is really the "best" she can get. Again, I want to emphasize that we're not going to get real heavy into all of these psycho-social phenomena and concepts of the like.

The full machinery of all of these dynamics, and what needs to be done to alter the course of time is very well entrenched in other texts, and so, a tour through not only *Solid 6*, but also the finalizing reference guide will rig you up with the well-rounded library for your shelf.

The core essence of *Solid 6* is to provide the struggling acolyte with a spread of simple and memorable rationale and strategy so that he can get his ass rolling *today*, and embark upon starting a regimen of regular interaction with women, and to maintain a reliable level of frequency of such that will make for an ample surfeit. I do believe truly, however, that the Game is cyclical – there will be stretches of time where the action will markedly taper down, and will do so no matter how hard you might try to fight it. It's just not meant to be played year around. You will need breaks, whether you want them or not, so learn to embrace them.

But once you know how the system works, and have the power to *work* the system, you'll be sure to see those valleys taper back toward peaks. In the grander scheme of things, the times when you're not dating at all will be due *you* choosing to stop, not because you just couldn't muster the cluster to build a new stable of leads.

A Note on Outliers

As you delve into the beholding and upholding of the principles and practices of *Solid 6*, you'll, of course, encounter stark exceptions to the rules, ultimately even prompting you to contort the boundaries of the rules. Perhaps in the hopes that tailoring your strategic parameters in favor of the proliferation of said outliers will widen your spectrum of prospects.

Please resist that probable inclination. Just because, for what proved to be one of your best dates so far, she had readily opted to travel twenty-five miles to meet you in your city, doesn't make for any kind of justification for you to try to typically leverage that practice from your leads.

We're *not* endeavoring to build a business off of outliers. It's like, upon hearing about a guy who built a multi-million dollar empire on sock-repair, and so, you're buoyed into becoming the next sock-repair millionaire, instead of investing your resources into some well established type of business. Just keep that in mind when those exceptions roll around, and they will. What you will set up as your consistently winning strategies should be strictly adhered to as often as you can manage.

Part Two

The 3 Pillars of Dating

Here I present the hefty bulk of *Solid 6*. The most comprehensive and pragmatic approach to dating that I've yet to see – the "3 Pillars of Dating" is an encompassment of wisdom that I've amassed over the course of my expeditions. Reminiscent of comparable contemporary philosophies, I feel that the 3 Pillars have a unique edge, given not only their simplicity, but also their inherent crispness and earthy perspective.

Indeed, it could be reasoned that each "pillar" is cobbled together with the blocks of many interrelated themes, and thus, smoothly grouped together in these three expansive categories. I've resisted the occasional inclination to devise a conceivable 4th or 5th pillar, and yet, I'll find myself melding such ideas back into one of the existing three.

Various frameworks of clauses, rules, or even outright commandments for our grappling with not only dating, but intersexual relations as a whole, offer us stacks of declarations to abide by. These layouts exist in various amounts. For just a couple of examples, such as Rollo Tomassi's "Iron Rules", of which there are nine, to even a good twenty, such as with Caleb Jones' list of rules for 1st dates. These are fine systems, and the bulk of what they profess ring true. However, at least as far as a system for dating is concerned, I dig the raw simplicity and utility of three – and you will too.

The paramount goal of the 3 Pillars is to fortify your position in the dating market into the strongest and safest that can be feasibly attained, within the limits of our current age. To be real, abiding by the 3 Pillars may not elevate you to *the most desirable state*, but still, it may very well prove to be the best deal you're gonna get.

Once we're well-versed in the preliminary concepts

and shit necessary in *acquiring* leads, and thus getting them to sit in front of you for actual dates (& you *will* get dates) – it's primarily within the confines of that interaction where the 3 Pillars really stand true as your guiding edifice.

Trust me, the 3 Pillars of Dating are time-tested and built of experience. Through the arduous endurance of a series of milestones, I've discovered the underlying principles on which the 3 Pillars are built. Upon 120+ dates' worth of experience (so far), the pillars have borne the weight of the cumulative lessons learned from such an expanse of interactions.

Let's look at the system which will govern your dating strategy . . .

The 1st Pillar – She's Replaceable

I realize that any dude with even a distant familiarization with Game/Red Pill awareness will find a recognizable chime here. You may even dismissively pocket this maxim, considering it an all ready central load-bearing tenet of your psyche. – and yet, recall how easily and frequently you've found yourself dreamily fixated on one particular girl who'd long since forgotten about you, and the mental meanderings you went through to try to figure out how to resurrect the affair.

Right now I'll take a side-bar real quick so I can note how the "she" in this pillar does have some contextual sensitivity. A mother, a sister, or even a wife of forty years can never be replaced. Those are women with a uniquely special merit. I mean, what makes any one person special to you? I'd hope it'd be a damn good justification. And so, in winding back to our central theme – that chick who you've become brazenly enamored with over the great big hour that you've known each other, but so soon after she's since vanished? Yeah, you can bet your fuckin' ass . . . she's replaceable. New leads make for the very air that Game breathes.

Keeping this rhetoric hammered in is gonna save you from a lot of problems. Ultimately, you will learn how to deduce the level of attraction a girl has for you, and most critically, when it tapers down into obliviousness. In the majority of instances, this whole process will go through within the confines of that 1st (and only) encounter. So, when that realization finally arrives that she's just not that into you, you'll know that you *must* simply jettison the "feelings" you had so quickly built for her . . . and then you can please refrain from sending her what would be the fifth consecutive, unanswered text.

The 2nd Pillar – Max the Interaction

Here we have the pillar that will require a certain perceptual ability to effectively utilize it. The foundational principle of the 2nd Pillar is that it is a prime objective of every one of your dates – every "interaction" – that you fully explore as to the degree of physical intimacy that can be feasibly achieved. Furthermore, this will be within the scope of that single *interaction*.

This has a lot of different implications, surely. As an abstract concept, there is *no limit* to the degree of intimacy one can achieve within the confines of even a single hour's date. You can meet a chick for coffee in a gentrified and public setting, starting off devoid of any physical contact . . . and eighty minutes later you've since coaxed her to enthusiastically be chained up in the sex-dungeon in your basement. There we go again with outliers, but the point I'm making with such a grandiose example is that the full spectrum is perfectly plausible. Don't ever doubt it.

Now, what I was referring to initially as a "perceptual ability" deals with the very real boundary that you will have to contend with, and that limit will exist, case-by-case, and will differ on each individual date. Over time, through repetition, you'll develop the ability to gauge how receptive she is in regard to the extent of intimacy she might want with you. Determining this will be a process that you calibrate your game to, based on certain cues, behaviors and impressions on her part. Upon *recognizing* the message telegraphed, covertly or otherwise, you will act accordingly, as you see fit.

As your acuity becomes increasingly honed, you'll be able to confidently and competently find out just how wide (or narrow) the goal posts are, within the confines of each individual date – as it will vary tremendously.

True mastery of the 2nd Pillar means walking away for a date *knowing* that you've wrung out every drop of physicality potential, *within* the established boundaries of her consensual desires, so that optimally, your mind will be devoid of any saddling regret of perhaps having "missed out" on something.

The ability is all about actually judging how receptive she is. Like an infrared scope revealing a path of lasers, her receptiveness to your advances won't be readily deducible to you if you've yet to acquire a certain level of perceptual acumen.

It's about finding out the range of those limits, but most critically, fully utilizing what those limits have to offer you to work with – maximizing the interaction.

Now, I'll pause there real quick to point out how I know that this implies some lofty, expansive potential to get raunchily sexual with every goddamn date. This is *not* the case. What the 2nd Pillar amounts to – its essence – is to acknowledge and explore that breadth of potential, within the set limit – regardless of its relative vastness. You'll do dates by where she doesn't want to be touched *at all*, and other instances where, really, your own apprehension may prove to be the only limiting factor. The point is that as long as you've established convincingly to yourself that you've nudged that outer reach of what you can do, even if finding that out took only a single move, then you'll have embraced the 2nd Pillar.

This could be simply a light touch on her hand, causing her to reflexively pull away. Or, another specific sort of "test" I'd stumbled upon is when I'm walking with her through a doorway or something, I'll take her by the waist, or place a hand on the small of her back, to see if she reacts negatively to such. I've had a few instances where she'd take this gesture quite quizzically, even asking me why I'm touching her, or just by pulling away. If you run into one of these admittedly rare instances where the girl *verbally* rebukes you for attempting such a rudimentary move, I'd strongly recommend you promptly find some pretext to excuse yourself from the interaction.

A more drawn out equivalent to that could be a case where your repeated efforts to close the physical proximity to her, scattered throughout that hour is met with a forcefield-like repulsion, then really, that shit's gonna go nowhere.

I know full well that, amidst your quests, abiding by the 2nd Pillar will invoke concerns of "pushing too far", thus potentially "blowing it" – a common trope I've heard from less enlightened men. Yes, indeed, she must have genuine desire for you, and we're not in the business of trying to radically change her mind. The objective is to merely nudge her along the direction she was *all ready* moving in the first place. As far as pushing too far or blowin' it and that kind of shit goes, I really wouldn't worry about it. A *far* more menacing hazard is that you'll end up not pushing hard enough.

I'm not saying that you'll never neutralize a prospect as a direct result of overstepping the bounds (you will), but the lesson here is that for every date, without exception, the *superior* state is where you've taken the gamble by testing the limit, maxed the interaction, devoid of any concern on your part as to any negative bearing it might have, or any potential for consequential interaction with that particular girl.

So, you went too "fast" for her, got busted, and "blew it". Who gives a fuck? You better have eight more leads in your phone.

The 3rd Pillar – It Doesn't Mean Anything to Her

In what could be interpreted as the most provocative – but *surely* not of a domineering value to the other two – the 3rd Pillar may very well prove to be the toughest to wrap your mind around. I know it's been for me, anyway.

Remember, the 3 Pillars are in balance and harmony. They compliment and fulfill each other, no one pillar towers over another. But each has a different composition, its own thematic emphasis. Each one requires a progression of realization in order to be fully understood and embraced. Each pillar needs the others in order to stand tall with full power.

The 1st Pillar strikes me as sporting a certain brevity and crispness. Its philosophy you can almost gulp in one bite – at least to understand its message. However, in true practice, it'll take major-league experience for you to learn your ass to take it to heart.

The 2nd Pillar wears a different set of colors, in that its emphasis is all about the development of a specific skill-set, as well as the gaining of proficiency in perceptive ability. And finally, the 3rd Pillar enmeshes you in a jungle-gym of oddity and wonderment, tempered by societal influence and psychological mystique.

Like the preceding two pillars, the very soul of the 3rd Pillar is beheld through true repetition and experience, and only through such will you be able to utilize it to its full and intended purpose - as a system for governing your dating adventures. *The 3 Pillars* was developed, realized and tailored exclusively for the optimal navigation of romantic endeavor on the introductory, casual level.

As you'll discover, each of the lessons the 3 Pillars will bestow upon you will likely make for a daunting pill to ingest. My own initial rubbing up on the 3rd Pillar goes back a good few years ago. I remember back to the time period where I was consistently practicing cold-approaching. Really, I was the fuckin' Terminator, hitting up any and every chick I deemed even remotely appealing, but even a lot of real stunners, diving right into the play, irrespective of intimidating beauty

Consequently, I'd put together a veritable phone book of numbers, what I'd comically term the "Necronomicon". Yeah, color me surprised as I found the vast majority of these numbers going absolutely nowhere, but even upon realizing such a prominent pattern, the sentiment would persist on my part that getting a chick's number was kind of *big* deal.

I'll have a chapter devoted to approach dynamics to be presented later, but for purposes of discussing the 3rd Pillar, I wanted to illustrate what proved to be a watershed event in my initial formulating of it, as it happened to have been mired in my big league approaching period.

A major percentage of that approaching took place at the university I was ~~wasting my time at~~ attending. One day, at a quad I spied a beautiful girl of the typical 18-21 age range you'd find in such a setting. I promptly seated myself at her table and initiated a general conversation about classes, and such, and she seemed fairly receptive. After no more than fifteen minutes, I snagged her number before departing (*dazzle*). What's more, she had disclosed to me how she just happened to live in my city. What were the chances? I'm sure you can figure I thought that I really "had something" there.

Over what I reckon was the next week or two, I texted her a couple of times, in the form of "what's up", or the like. Not to be deterred by the complete absence of any response, I took one more swing at it, and surely, the 3rd time proved to be the charm. It was September of '15, standing at my kitchen counter when, right after I'd sent that last text, the phone lit up with an incoming call from   RESTRICTED. The second's worth of enthusiasm slaked just as fast as it had appeared.

The cholo-sounding kid on the other end turned out to be the chick's boyfriend, and in the predictable fashion, he played it tough, admonishing me for contacting her, followed, by a repeatedly authoritative sneer to "stop texting her". At no point did I remind him of the underlying condition that brought this situation about – that being "his" girl handing off the digits to random dudes. No, I'm afraid I was too occupied with meekly folding like a subservient napkin, even lamely feigning ignorance as to who I was messaging in the first place, but still pledging to comply with this crassly proposed demand.

He seemed appeased at that point, and hung up. I put the phone down on the counter, in a fearful silence. Up to that point, the bulk of the wealth of numbers I'd amassed went nowhere, really, or perhaps a few enduring exchanges. But what was this? I'll tell you what it was. A long in coming realization that, in this day and age at least, getting a chick's number ain't worth a dead dog's asshole. It's as close to nothing without actually being as such.

It was quite profound, really. This minute instance hammered that home. From that point on, finally, I was prompted to lift the improper load of weight I'd been instinctively and reflexively sitting upon the value of getting the stupid fuckin' number. The mere first cornerstone of the pillar had been set.

I even remember now, of the several times I'd throw a recently acquired number through Facebook, and the chick's profile would spring up, and bam, right on the main profile pic, she'd be there with her boyfriend or equivalent, but she'd handed me her number like some cheap trinket.

Realize how back before the predominance of cell phones, a girl giving you her number had quite the bulky implication to it, as it'd mean you'd likely ring up a household, and *someone* would have to actually talk to you, while today, your inquiry will likely mingle amongst all her other calls, or just get dumped right into her blocked list.

Without getting into an expansive analysis of why girls give out their stupid number to guys they have zero interest in, we're merely going to acknowledge and highlight the main point being that it doesn't mean anything to her – the "it" in this specific context being her giving you the number.

Nor are we to embark upon some sort of enlightenment campaign to inform women at large as to the erroneousness of such a practice. Nay, and nay again. The one and only important thing is for you to simply take them as they are and run with it. Personal success will be achieved only through the fostering of change from within.

Oh, did you think that this stops at the phone number bullshit? The realm of the 3rd Pillar is just getting rolling at this point. Let's further explore the somber insight to be found with this pillar.

It wouldn't be for a couple more years after I'd endured the "number" realization, when I'd be doing dating to any kind of regular degree of prevalence. Step-by-step, by way of raw immersion and repetition, through the encountering of certain "milestones", would I learn how all of this rhetoric and strategy swings in reality.

I remember one of the earliest dates, in what would ultimately prove to be simply one of a very extensive succession of different dates. A generic white girl in her late 30s, she lived around twenty miles from me, and actually volunteered the notion of meeting me at a venue that lay halfway in between our respective locations. I've since learned that such a proposal is a rarity. My standards for "excellence" amidst these earlier dates especially, were quite meager. I was only so still amazed that this average whatever chick was readily available to meet me. So, in the spirit of our 3rd Pillar discussion, I think this might've been the first instance where I held hands with a chick. Our interaction, of a middling quality, consisted of conversing at a table of a popular bar, where we also shared drinks and a small plate. As we ventured into the parking lot I made the lofty gambit of reaching for her hand. She reciprocated in kind, and if I can properly recall, the interaction was topped off with my meek inquisition for a kiss, which was softly rebuffed.

The point here is how I distinctly recollect how, given the hand-hold, I felt an almost subconscious zap, by where I was gripped with the impression that I really "had something" there. We threw a few texts back and forth after that, but she ultimately faded away.

It would take way more hand-holds for me to finally graduate past that rudimentary bullshit and to keep pushing, garnering the realization that it just doesn't mean anything to her.

As I stated previously, no *one* pillar stands at a superior importance to the others, though lemme tell ya, the 3rd one seems to offer me the most bewilderment, even up to the present time. It simply astounds me still, how with tight game, expertly applied to a receptive chick, the spectrum of "stuff" you can do with her, sending her into a passionate whirlwind, leaving you convinced that she's been enraptured – only for her to disappear upon the hour's end, never to return.

Milestones. Interval by interval, I would experience definitive interactions where a tangible realization would dawn on me, enlightening my clarity in understanding (and accepting) the very fundamental principles that govern all of these interactions.

I'm reminiscing now, to yet another such "milestone date". June of '18. Another average-y, decently attractive, slim white girl, 34, with a rather unique job, as some sort of archeologist. By this time period I had since learned the importance in picking a venue *right* in the girl's area in order to optimize the likelihood of the date's occurrence. Anyway, so I picked a place that I don't reckon was more than a bare mile from her place. Surely, such a strategy serves many purposes, as will be discussed later.

Finding parking in the Echo Park region of Downtown LA was agonizing. I damn near gave up and took off, but just in time for the date, I managed it. Minutes upon my arrival at the front of the venue, she arrived, and I was very pleased at how she looked. The place was some lil' corner eatery – now I'll just be the one to stop the story right there, so you can sling a noose around my fucking neck so I can swing from the gallows for a taking a chick out to *eat* – and during the day no less. I didn't know much better at the time, so let's just get over it.

Certainly, the food was more palatable than the conversation, as I distinctly recall how, during the date, I had been prompted to mull over in my mind, how she must've been "having none of it", as I gauged her level of enthusiasm for my end of the deal as being sub-optimal.

I think I ended up choosing to pay for us both (*gasp!*), and I prepared to walk her to where she'd parked, across a very wide city street. Upon getting there, I figured that'd be the end of it, but she seemed to linger for a sec, and so, I stepped forward for an embrace, followed by a kiss – an unorthodox move, considering how there had been virtually no progression of physical escalation up to that point.

To my surprise, she readily reciprocated, in what amounted to a fifteen-minute make-out right there in the middle of the sidewalk, along the busy intersection. It purveyed in seemingly perpetual intervals of kissing, and to a caliber of passion I had yet at that time to be acquainted with.

Each of these episodes was followed by a kind of furtive pause, predominantly initiated by myself, as a mundane show of modesty, anytime people walking the sidewalk neared us. But after, I'd re-engage, kissing her neck, feeling and groping her ass, through her yoga pants.

After so many rounds of this, at long last we mustered the resolve to finally part from each other's most immediate proximity. As we took a few steps opposite from one another, I capstoned the exchange by reaching forth and softly grabbing one of her breasts.

As a bluff, really, I beckoned her to permit me to follow her back to her place, to which she declined, after some hesitation, claiming a mixed sentiment of latent guilt for appearing too "easy", as well as her roommate likely being home. And so, as she climbed into her car, I leaned on a wall, and waved her off, in a display of being playfully dismissive.

I was parked back across the street, and I as I crossed back through that massive intersection, I was seized with, likc, a pang of apprehension. The thought struck me, "Oh wow. This chick is gonna want something serious. This is big. Fuck, I'm gonna have to commute down here regularly and blah-blah . . ."

Maybe you can take a guess as to where all this went. Within the hour of returning home, she texts me with a hefty version of "The Speech" (slang with which you'll become all-too familiar with yourself), where she claimed to not know why she did all that, and how she didn't "see this going anywhere". To this array of astonishing perplexity, I responded, "'k".

You can see by that, how I was somewhat primed for this type of outcome, but I was still tilted by it. It was a milestone moment, to be sure. All of that amorous, physical intimacy. A world-class colossus of an event for me . . . but, I suppose, just some fleeting, whatever bullshit for her. It didn't *mean anything*. I remember that date brought the first serious inclination for me to quit.

I was mystified. I was frustrated. Why didn't it mean anything to her? Why *doesn't* it mean anything to her? Now, one could devote a whole book to that question, but here, I'll take the brisk way out by citing a notion that you'll see referenced often amongst these pages – she has too many options.

Yes, yes, I realize that every individual's circumstances are unique, and there could be a wealth of reasons as to why an interaction with a chick went nowhere, but let me simply provide you with a rationale that, although may not satiate your need for answers, it'll give you some peace . . . she has too many options.

In our current age, any and every one of 'em is just so saturated with complimentary attention, prospective suitors, and free license to explore her sexuality and agency that, simply put, no *one* guy is gonna do it for her, at least not for long. Do you think you'll be the coolest, toughest, baddest guy she's *ever* met? Well, if you did, I'd praise your self-assuredness, but if that proves not to be the case, please try to wrangle your reflexive response when she vanishes after that hour's romp. She's not gonna traipse into the 6,300-flavors ice cream shop, and exit with but a single cone. Or five.

I should illustrate now that the rhetoric of the 3rd Pillar is not limited to physical intimacy. No, no, it gets even better. Any degree of emotional or personality connection you may have formed with her, whatever spread of common interests you both turned out to share . . . that's right – it doesn't mean anything to her.

This makes me think of yet another date with a generic, lanky white girl who turned out to be quite savvy in the computer field, a scene in which I had spent a good number of years. In abiding by the 2nd Pillar, I had deduced that she was *not* receptive to any level of physical escalation past the most superficial touching, so I hung back on all that. But I optimistically figured that our unusual commonalities would shine through, and she'd entertain my presence for a longer-than-average time stretch.

The next day, in a leisurely response to my second date pitch text, she offered an exceptional, "double-barreled" rejection. Initially consisting of a more typical version of "The Speech", but after I responded with a "that's cool", she was obviously perturbed by how dismissive I was, and so she shot back a second text, laced with this sort of phony sanctimoniousness, plying me with the notion of "how painful it must be for you to be rejected like this".

Seriously. I (unnecessarily) texted back how I've been through that enough times to warrant a decent level of immunity to it, so . . . fuckin' whatever. I should've just deleted it, or even told her to get over herself. Shit.

The raw and real truth of that response was indeed how, by then I'd heard that little ditty a good two hundred times, so I could give a fuck. The important thing was that I'd acquired "immunity". In time, you will too. If, in truth, it really doesn't mean anything to her, then it shouldn't to *you*.

Part Three
Online & Offline

I'll start off what will proceed to be (sigh) a major component of *Solid 6* with a disclaimer that I'll be making few, if any friends amidst "the community" for being an advocate for online game. I know, I know, dating apps are a garbage bin of single moms, fatties, psychotic, burned-out spinsters and all the like. Well, yeah – they are. But at least this dumpster's lid is unlocked and flung open for you. And more than that, it will offer you what live approaching may not be – accessibility.

I'm gonna pause right here to underline the tantamount importance of engaging in live approaching on a usual basis, and in a virtual fantasy world, this avenue would be your predominant method of meeting chicks – with online being relegated to a distant supplementary role, and ideally, even being phased out into obsolescence.

However, back to the Earth's surface, to reality, and likely *your* reality, you're fairly riddled with angst over making plays, and even if you are prolific at it, maybe you tend to get a bit vexed upon being ignored or told "I have a boyfriend" for the 2,700[th] time. So we're gonna delve into what these apps, which seem to be the big thing now, have to offer. And they *can* offer you dates of a level of overall quality that *you* would deem acceptable

To start on this, I do realize that, given the technological dynamics of this arena, that I run the risk of devoting focus to material that may become antiquated at a later time period. The effectiveness of the *specific*, step-by-step roadmap I'm gonna provide for you, to get new leads *tonight* may not hold up indefinitely. I don't think we need to worry about that possibility, though, since the underlying principles of this entire study are virtually timeless themselves, and also, these apps have been around for two decades and surely, they will persist as a standard for some years to come.

I've seen very few publications devoted to providing a with-the-times, minutely detailed guide to getting consistent results through online dating. What I'll present here, I'd hope will prove to be a foundational guide that's denuded of the more typical raining down on dudes who opt to fuck with the stupid apps. I'm not gonna admonish you to "get out there, be confident, and talk to chicks". Truly, I would *never* dissuade you from making plays, but if we're to get real and serious, it'd be in your best overall interests to utilize your every available avenue. So let's get on the heavy goulashes and hip-waders, and trudge . . .

We'll launch this roadmap by familiarizing you with a couple of key tenets to online dating. The most paramount of which is that the very *last* thing a woman is looking for on a dating app . . . is a date. Huh? I thought this was a dating site? What about all these chicks on there bemoaning about wanting "something serious"? Well, that's cute talk and all, but lemme tell you what they're lookin' for – attention. A great shame of the online scene is how it's so chock full of these mediocre-ass chicks who, as they're out and about throughout the day, probably don't get too much affirmation and validation of their sense of value, step into a new world once they log onto their dating app profiles.

A limitless cavalcade of achingly thirsty imbeciles, peppering her with free attention, consequently boosting her ego to artificially stratospheric heights. A consistent regimen of that will get her to think that she's really some special shit after all – and certainly too good for your pedestrian ass. She can hold out for a while longer, filter out the likes of you, without even having to leave the house, sit back and let the "offers" roll in.

So, keeping that in mind will prime you for the type of muck you're gonna slosh through. The other key tenet of online dating I need for you to be familiar with is that online you'll encounter *all* of the worst and *none* of the best. The majority of the very lowest quality chicks you'll ever meet will be from off of apps. Not to say you won't encounter terrible women in live approaches, but it's easier to deduce one's personality and the like straight off in person, as opposed to what can be gleaned from an online profile. You'll scope out chicks on there that appear to be decent, score a date, and find the deal to be not quite as cool as you thought it was.

Conversely, you just won't find the top-tier chicks on these apps. They're just not on there – and why should they be? Chicks on that level simply have no serious inclination to bother with that shit. Among their immediate peer circle, social media accounts, and throughout the day's travels, the banquet of attention she's getting outta provide an ample supply.

So please, keep that fact in mind to help ensure your motivation to hit the streets, the Sprouts, Trader Joe's, Whole Foods, and the college campus, so that you can try to access the rest of the women.

One of the dimmest consequential effects of online dating usage is a sort of tunnel-vision, where you get to think "that's all there is", until you go back outside to a public forum where chicks congregate, and you realize, "Oh wow, there're the ones I'm talkin' about. Where the hell are *they* on this damn site?"

The distinction can appear so pronounced, it's as if women online are from some other planet. But they're not.

They're just more women. When you browse online, that whole crowd on there is in your immediate attention span, and while they're out there in real life interaction, you're simply not so prone to notice them, your field of vision being naturally tailored to whatever you happen to like most.

Selecting Apps/Building Your Profile

Now that we're committing ourselves to the folly of getting down to this online bullshit, we can at least be assured that it'll be played out in the most efficient and effective manner possible. We'll try to minimize the time to dump into it, while maximizing the feasible results.

I've been using these apps intermittently since 2012, and in that stretch, I've noticed certain transitions and patterns in trends, which is part of what's led me to formulate the blueprint strategy to be presented here. I'll underscore a few instances by where certain methods and practices were effective in the past, but have since lost their efficacy. This'll prove critical, as adhering to archaic strategy will not only fail to generate leads, you'll waste fuckin' time.

I categorize dating apps/sites into two camps, with a couple of sub-divisions I'll note later. These broadest of categories are *paid* and *free* apps. Paid apps have a required admission price for membership for the user to be able to utilize any worthwhile function of the site (ie: messaging), while free apps permit the necessary gamut of functions required to generate leads. Also, virtually every free app has "paid features", ostensibly to "unlock" additional options for the user. Finally, there are what I call "niche apps" that cater to special populations, and come in both the paid and free flavors. I'll do a quick critique on the spread of apps I've tried, but fortunately, the bulk of the strategies to be found here will be universally applicable.

As much as I should discourage you from even fucking with this online shit, and yet, we're gonna do it anyway, *I will*, however, draw the line in regards to any free app, *strongly* recommending you to not bother with them. They truly are garbage. Maybe a while back they had some endearing value, but presently, it's just too slanted as a shameless waste.

The main reason for this is that on the free apps there's just too much shit to wade through and not nearly enough of any kind of prize to even be had for the work. Remember when I talked about how there's an upward limit to the quality of chicks on these things? See, this isn't the case for dudes. *Every* swingin' hog is cruisin' these apps, at some span of time or another, thus guaranteeing that for any one lame-ass chick's attention, you'll be runnin' up against everyone from drifters to members of royal houses – a tremendous "hive" of messages constantly buzzing around each chick's profile. You can be a fuckin' CK model, and it'd still be likely your damn opener message will never be seen.

And as if that weren't enough, since it's a free app, the overall population of users will be far greater than a paid app, since, well, it's fuckin' free. If nothing else, a paid app filters out (a little), not only some dinks that you'd otherwise have to run up against, but also, some chicks who are even less "serious" than those investing a fuckin' admission price.

Topping all of this off, I will note what's possibly the most important distinction between a paid and a free app – there's simply *far* too many fake/dead profiles, scammers, bots, hookers, and transsexuals on free apps. It's a mess.

Oh, and I almost forgot – if you think that tapping into

a free app's paid features might remedy any of that shit, you'd be mistaken. After you've slammed down the green, that same shit "talent" will be there waitin' for you, along with that army of competitors. Being granted the option of seeing if a chick read your message, or getting a "boost", or any of that other type of shit is valueless. Don't bother.

Later on I'll present a brief assessment of the apps I've actually used, so as to better prep you for what you should be fuckin' around on. For right now that won't matter, as we're gonna just get rolling on the preliminary dynamics that are universally applicable.

Get out the scratch you'll need for your stupid membership fee and set it on the desk. You're not gonna be using it quite yet. We need to take care of something first – something that the *vast* majority of guys aren't gonna bother with. And that is to get pro photos. I'm gonna say it again – get . . . pro . . . photos. If your lame ass ain't up for that shit, then stay the fuck off these damn apps. I know what you're gonna want to do – slap together some bullshit, using whatever old dogshit pix of yourself, uninspired selfies and cliché gym/in-car shots. Or, better still, photos of yourself at a *much* younger age or lighter weight range. Yeah, that's right, it's not just chicks who are habitually guilty of that practice.

Pull any of that shit, and you can just go ahead and blend right into the rest of the sub-par male crowd, and telegraph to every chick you message that you're not gonna bother with the effort, and she should just adore your ass as-is.

Showcasing professionally arranged photos yields the dual benefit of not only displaying value to women by proving that you're putting in an attentive effort in the display you're all ready paying for, but also, you're maximizing your appearance through snappy and stylized poses, making optimized usage of such factors as lighting, wardrobe, and setting. A spread of competently compiled photos that give you an aura of gritty mystique, or an alluring persona can substantially compensate for a level of attractiveness that might be less than stellar.

Never lose sight of the fact that *every* chick on there is getting a constant bombardment of messages, and though, given that, she may very well not happen to uncover your shot out from under the bottom of the pile, the ones she does latch onto will be only the best.

Go on Craigslist or whatever and hire a pro photographer, or even find a photography student to recruit. I had stumbled upon what turned out to be a high school kid's posting on NextDoor, offering a generous shoot for *$15*. Took care of my first attempt at providing proper photos.

All right . . . I imagine it's been several weeks (or more), but you finally got around to getting the damn photos. Now you can register for membership. Do *not* pay for more than one month's worth. We'll get into why in a bit, but for now, just heed this. Ignore the enticements of discounts. One month. If a paid app requires a longer term minimal, *don't* use that app. Once you've signed the fuck on, slam those pix on there.

Ok . . . as far as what to *write* on one of these things, there're varying schools of thought, including a stance of not even putting anything on there – the full brunt of the weight laying on your pix. I'd be comfortable endorsing this approach, given as to how in the realm of online dating – just as elsewhere, it's all about looks, so let's just get *with it*, and put your best self forward.

As for myself, I typically do assemble just a snappy

lil' profile description, onto which I toss additional lines over time, as I think of them. Something along the lines of, say, vaguely alluding to what you're "looking for on here", some fluffy quips that display that you're fun to be around, interesting, cool, and most importantly – *normal*. Chicks have an innate sense for perceiving "weirdness", and if that needle on the meter even trembles, you're *out*. Keep that in mind throughout, and especially at this stage of the process, where you're decidin' on what to put in your profile, like your hobbies and shit. I'm not gonna make any suggestions, but if you even remotely surmise that a particular pursuit of yours or aspect of yourself might be taken as odd by a chick, *don't put that shit* in your goddamn profile. And don't put anything in there that could be construed as self-deprecating, or even the slightest hint that you're some kind of a drag. This is all I'm gonna venture to offer ya on that.

Now that you've got your profile set up, we next move onto another, entirely critical component of online dating, and one, in addition to the photos, is a factor that most guys fuck up . . . messaging.

Who should you message? *What* do you message? Should you even message in the first place? That's right – one of my favorite coaches, Corey Wayne, in his passing reference to how you should approach the online scene, advocates, in short, putting together a profile that's sufficiently intriguing and alluring as to actually prompt chicks to message *you* first. Upon receiving such inquiries, you're to send her *your* number (he sez he doesn't "waste time" sending chicks messages).

This layout may very well be the *one* and only piece of his advice that I completely disagree with. Fuck, maybe in 2003 this worked, or some shit, but today I'd be a bit curious as to scope out a bro's inbox after a month on that plan.

I'll take this opportunity to quickly comment how, periodically, you'll run into chicks who counter *your* initial asking for her number by requesting that you give her yours. Fuck that. Play that game, and you won't hear from her, and even if you did, you won't meet. Your policy towards all this kind of shit should be, "If you don't comply, good-bye".

Now, if you have *stunning* looks and physique, hell, I bet any goddamn plan can be leveraged, but for the reader sitting right here, I'm gonna let you in on a lil' trade secret – you will get *zero* unsolicited messages, and even if you did, they'd be from chicks you don't want one from.

The format that *you* will use for your messaging will be a sort of hybrid of two different methodologies. The first of these being composing a message that's uniquely tailored to the content in her profile VS. a "cut & paste" opener. What both approaches have in common is that you'll be doing them a lot, and in a short a burst of time as you can manage. You want to sprawl out as wide a net as you can. Realize that the probability of any one message being replied to is nearly zero, so it's imperative to blast off as many of these fellas as possible.

As far as the raw effectiveness goes, in comparing the "tailored message" format VS. "cut & paste", I really couldn't be conclusive about it. If a given chick who bit onto your custom message would've done so on a generic opener, who the hell knows? The integral factor is to just get her attention so that she can pause for two seconds to scope out your pix – the true hook.

Through heavy experimentation with both methods, I've indeed arrived at a certain resolve – and that's to lean more in the direction of the cut & paste opener, but one with a certain flair and structure that I'll elaborate on in a bit. The main reason why I ultimately opted for cut/paste is simply time and ease – it's *far* more important to be able to send off as big a sheer volume of messages as you can, in as little time as you can, than it is to try to appeal to a given woman's flimsy likelihood of taking note of your sentimentality to her "uniqueness". A quick caveat though – in utilizing the "cut & paste" format, you will *not* slam out a barrage of messages made up of "Hey", "whats up", "how's your day going?", and certainly not, "Oh my god, you're so beautiful". Women hate that, and surely there's no better way to fade back into the crowd of online losers.

For you to run your "quota" for the day, or whatever measure of time you endeavor upon, you need to prioritize expediency, efficiency, and effectiveness. Now then, I'll present the definitive structure for not only running a quota's worth of messaging, but also for the navigation and review of profiles on a dating app.

I'll show you the opener I've taken quite the preference to typically use, as it has proven to yield some unique value for a few reasons. Certainly, you can come up with your own, as there's surely no "magic" opener that'll really shine through. Still, they ain't all the same . . .

Let's plan our 1st date.

Bam. I'll message this to fifty chicks I like the look of, within twenty minutes, log off, done for the day. Note how I said "like the *look* of". This means that I go on no other evaluations (yet), such as bothering to read the stupid profiles, and furthermore, I even take the gamble of going off of that one cover pic. This is all to facilitate not only brevity and smoothness, but also to help foster *results*. Casting that wide net quickly, getting her attention quickly, all while pissing away the minimal amount of time is paramount.

We'll pause to take a closer look at that opener, so that you can see why I feel it has a certain effectiveness. Firstly, it's a statement. We're not asking her anything. We're *telling* her we should plan our first date. Secondly, by offering to plan "our 1st date", there's the clear implication of subsequent dates, thus sporting an admirable confidence straight off. Thirdly, we're referring to our tentative encounter as a *date*, not a "meet-up", a "meet & greet", or any of that weak shit – and there *is* a distinction. Getting plied with such artificial propositions is among the assorted hazards you'll occasionally encounter, and I'll show you how to deal with them.

And lastly, the definitive nature of this opener has proven, surprisingly, to suss out chicks that are totally full of shit as far as actually leaving the house goes. You'll get chicks who'll respond very angrily to this opener, and good, 'cause you'll know right there that you're done with her, but it might be tough, admittedly, to tamp out your momentary enthusiasm at the fact that a chick actually responded (snort).

Conversely, and the majority of the time, chicks will be quite taken aback and elated at the directness of your approach – and bite onto it, hoping you'll continue to lead the exchange. Here's what you want your chatlog to look like, within the confines of the app . . .

Let's plan our 1st date.

Oh wow, that was fast, lol.
What'd you have in mind?

> We could do drinks or a scenic
> walk. Pass me your number,
> and we'll get rolling.

#

Or even better, I've been experimenting with a more "extensive" opener that beckons for the chick's number in *one* shot. So far though, it seems that, typically, they need to "warm" to you just over a message or two in order to feel out your vibe, heh, as much as could be deciphered through a coupla damn messages.

Why is this crispness so important? Well, for one, she's got the attention span of a mosquito, and in the two minutes it took you to get through that dash of back and forth, she just got another twenty-five messages. Never forget that. You want to cut through the horseshit and elevate yourself to the minority status of guys she actually hands the digits to – so you can then upgrade your ass to the phone.

Before we elaborate on what to do once you've got the digits, and ultimately set up and play through the date, lemme show you an example of a chatlog you *don't* want to see . . .

> Let's plan our 1st date.

> What?! We haven't even met
> yet! Is this what you tell all
> the girls . . . blah-blah-blah,
> bling-bling-bling, blah . . .

- OR -

<table>
<tr><td>Let's plan our 1st date.</td><td>We should get to know each other on here first.</td></tr>
</table>

Those instances, which you will run into often, are *dead shit*. They're nothing. You can take a jerk-boy swing at 'em by simply saying "What's your number?" repeatedly, but really, these are chicks you won't be meeting. I know that the second exchange, where the girl wants to talk "on here first" looks enticing, but I *guarantee* you, that if you foolishly opt to oblige her in this, your ensuing "conversation" will have a life expectancy of maybe two more messages, tops, before she fades away. She doesn't want to meet you, or anyone else on there for that matter. Simply delete these messages and roll the fuck on. Think of the apps as a mere staging platform where you browse through the action, "ping" you who like, get their numbers, and get off. To cleanly summarize, if she tries to *spar* with you over handing off the number, you've got nothing.

Out of more than a hundred online dates, shit, maybe three of 'em I pulled off through a big, drawn out chat on the app. All of the rest – you know how those came to be.

Going back to my proposition that you not even bother to read the profiles or scope out the subsequent pix manifests a certain gamble, I know. You might not have been able to tell that she's enormously fat (of which there's a robust chance), based on that main profile pic, which shows only her face, taken at an upward angle. Or that she has 17 kids, with a bevy of exes closely circling in tow. You know what – who gives a fuck?

What you're gonna do is merely wait until you get *a response*, and only then, scope out the profile in depth, and if you find something objectionable, delete the message. This kind of thing will come up occasionally, but the expediency of this format is well worth it. The best of a bad situation, anyway.

One more quick tipster I'll add, in regards to when you're at the point where it's warranted to look over her profile. If, throughout the spread of pix, her weight appears to fluctuate, *guarantee* that if you do opt to meet her, she'll be at her absolute heaviest. A good rule to go by is that if it looks like she's hiding something, she is. Just keep all that in mind before you decide to step out the door.

I realize that some of this shit you'd think would strike dudes as common knowledge, but the astonishment persists as to just how deplorable most guys' game is on these fuckin' apps, not to even mention out on the street. To a sufficient degree as to prompt the female administrators of those sites – with the help of their feminized, male white-knight counterparts, to periodically institute various restrictions, and "anti-chode" functions, as I call 'em, as scolding measures to come to the rescue of the poor female users at large from being harangued and victimized. We'll try to capitalize on all this further, primarily by proving to be among that minute percentage of men who aren't ravenously thirsty imbeciles.

I'll take a quick sidebar here to reference back to the notion of not exceeding one month's subscription at a time. The main reasoning behind that is the fact that by using this "canvassing" strategy, you'll certainly torch through everything listed on there in between three to ten days. Now, factors having to do with your own tastes as well as acceptable mileage radius will affect this, but still, in the grand scheme of things, there's not really a lotta chicks on these things.

Even with how mainstream online dating has become, there's still that lingering stigma it has as being some last resort refuge of the sub-par. I do feel that today this stigmatization has been sizably dampened, though still, when you see these chicks appear (and reappear) on these apps, and spread across a multitude of apps simultaneously, you're prompted to wonder, "What the hell's her problem? Just pick a guy and be done with it." The full scope of that discussion goes way past that of this book, as you can figure.

Ok, going back to the subscription term thing, the other reasons to not exceed a month's tour is that after you've exhausted the "talent" it will still take several weeks at least for it to regenerate, thus making it an even more grievous waste of money than it all ready is.

As a final suggestion, you ought not to be touring this shit year-round anyway, lest you want to become afflicted with chronic burn-out, as well as let erode whatever aptitude and inclination you might have at approaching. Go out for a month or two and make some fuckin' plays. Look sharp.

A Month's Tour – By the Numbers

Let's take a look at what kind of stats you should be aiming for within a standard month's touring, and the results you can expect from such. We'll also get into some of the general parameters for scheduling and structuring dates.

Solid 6

Subscription term: 1 month
Messages sent: 1,000-1,300
Reciprocity: 1%-5%
Leads: Approx. 20
Dates: 2-8

Sounds promising, huh? A lot of messaging there. The term "lead" or "prospect" I append to a girl whose number you got *and* she responded back to your text/call, as there will be plenty of instances to the contrary (and you will *not* try to keep messaging her!). So, in further analyzing those figures, a daily quota of around fifty messages – and this will stagger downward as you torch through the crowd – will amount to anywhere between several hundred to well over a thousand messages hammered out, with an overall response expectancy of 1% to 5%.

Out of a decent amount of those replies, you will get the number, while the rest will be "one-hit wonders" who message back once, and with an apparent enthusiasm, but quickly vanish right after, and the others being bullshitters who just want to "talk first on the site", and finally, the worst category, being those women who, in their misguided sense of courtesy, respond back merely to tell you how they're not interested, and to wish you good luck in your goddamn search. Let me just say again how much I *hate* that.

So . . . in total, you should be doing between two and eight dates a month. If your current results are all ready better than this, please send me *your* book, 'cause I could use it.

If that's not the case, however, we can now move on to learning the process of how to transition that stable of leads into actual dates. Getting her fuckin' ass in your real-life presence is the *only* product of any value. Messaging is shit.

Numbers are shit. Texting is shit. Video-calling, eh, some progress there . . . but still shit.

Earlier I hinted at the importance of getting her *off* of the app and "upgrading" the exchange to the phone. The primary purpose for this is, of course, is that the whole time you're still enmeshed with her in the realm of the app, the absolutely staggering cavalcade of other guys' messages you'll have to compete with will likely neutralize the exchange very quickly. It's an established fact that online (in contrast to real-life interaction), chicks hand off their number to only a rather minute percentage of dudes, so when you see that set of digits, know that you've been granted a very temporary, but critical promotion. You need to exploit this to the fullest and the fastest. This is not only due to the likelihood that, in three minutes, she'll fade out on you since she found someone else she likes even better, but also, by implementing this marked expediency, you have a decent chance of scoring a date *that hour*.

In order to help you adopt this mindset of spontaneity, I'm gonna prompt you to shed some of the "conventional wisdom" you might have all ready heard of, regarding just what to do with a girl's number once you get it. All the yap about how ya gotta wait two days, or five days, or ten days, or three years, so as to prevent yourself from being perceived as needy, or to "stand out from other guys" is simply archaic now. Period. In the time it took me to write this paragraph, she just got another fifty messages, so pick whether you're gonna text or call her, and do it right when you get the number, if you're really not otherwise occupied – which you won't be for this.

Yeah, yeah, you wanna put out the vibe that you're all busy and shit, on a mission and all that, but one of these pursuits of yours is getting leads and closing them, fast. You can worry about convincing her of your stellar value once you've met – which will likely be one time. So, set up that damn date, and be *ready* for those instances where she's up to meet right away.

That notion prompts me to cover another vitally important part of managing leads – logistics. When you set your search preferences for browsing, sit down and really think about how much traveling you're willing to do to see a chick that may not only disappoint your expectations, but surely, in all likelihood you'll never see again. As a novice, there's tremendous benefit to "fodder dates", that really serve no other purpose than building experience and exposure, but driving fifty miles to meet *any* chick is not only damn stupid, but a default display of low value. As if, really, you can't find enough leads within your nearest metropolitan area? Sure you can.

The very farthest I've traveled for a date was around forty-five miles. A "Solid 6", recently divorced Ukrainian chick, I met her for coffee at a location that couldn't have been more than a mile from where she lived. A pleasant enough interaction in the coffee place, tempered with instances of light and playful touching segued into a progression of passionate make-outs as we traipsed around the surrounding outdoor shopping center. I knew I had maxed the interaction upon her adamant halting at my series of attempts at either reaching down the back of her slacks or up inside her blouse.

See, I think it *might* have been possible to keep seeing her, had she lived much closer, but not withstanding the repeated effort that such would require of us (mainly for me), merely the existence of that sheer distance provided for just one more excuse for her to fade out on me. The 3 Pillars.

Swinging back to the true essence of this topic, I'll declare for you now that whatever city of residence you see stated on the girl's profile . . . you're *going* there for the date. Yes, there'll be isolated instances you'll be daring enough to coax her to your area, or a half-way, or she'll even suggest this, but that'll all be a minority percentage. You need to *default* on expecting to go to *her* area to meet. She wants this arrangement to occur with as little effort as possible – and you're gonna want to provide that convenience for her. In the greater expanse of the deal, a woman who is genuinely interested in you will "help" you in facilitating opportunities for interaction, but at this earliest stage, please, *please* be prepared to go right to her fucking neighborhood for the date, and raise *no* objection about it with her.

As we progress in this "digits-to-date" sequence, the emphasis so far has been about how to most efficiently get as many leads as quickly as possible, along with some key logistical strategy. From this point, I'd like to further detail steps such as how you should "regard" a number once you get it, selecting the venue, and a quick commentary on how to play out the actual date.

There's a lotta yap still, in the literature, about the "call VS. text" argument, as well as the time frame as to when you should first contact her. Roosh, as well as some other authors take care of this rather adequately, but I do want to throw in my own perspective on this.

I feel, very unfortunately, that many facets of Game have become "diluted" over the recent years, so that the raw of potency some of these practices once had is simply no longer evident. I think the aforementioned dynamic is a fine example of this.

The stance that, as an initial bid to stand out from other guys, you should always call her as opposed to texting, and as such only once some arbitrary delay period has elapsed. Just shit-can this. It may have made for an edge some time in the past, but today, such a trifle will create no sway in entertaining her good graces. Really, if out of her last one-hundred prospective suitors (no shit), seventy texted her, and the other thirty called, or even a ninety/ten slant, y'know, who gives a fuck? When you first get the fuckin' number, if you're in a particularly festive mood, call. Otherwise, just fuckin' text and set the damn thing up.

That leads me to a point that, at last, we can all agree on – the phone is for planning dates and that's it. Regardless of if you met her all ready through an approach or online, no jokes, flirting, stories, or whatever through text or any of that shit. The phone is the get-her-ass-in-front-of-you device.

Venues . . . venues. Once again, I'm gonna depart from the Manosphere/pick-up, etc. crowd by advocating a wider expanse of venue selection than you may be used to being "permitted" to utilize. In my research, I've certainly endured my share of hammering as to how you absolutely *must* take her "for drinks", and at night, and no lunch dates, no coffee dates, no dates in the daytime, blah-blah-blah.

If I were a chiseled stud who amassed 17,000 dates a year with 19-year-olds, I could justify such a meticulous exclusivity. Remember, if you're anywhere near that caliber, this book is fuckin' training wheels for you.

Anywho, back toward the less affluent neighborhood we're languishing in, I will take a sec to underscore yet another point in the literature I *do* wholly endorse. A given date should cost between zero and fifteen dollars. Most of my dates cost nothing (not even gas money every once in a great while). But lemme tell ya, before I started to *finally* get wise as to how to play this shit, the costs were all over the place. Terrible. And it didn't facilitate success worth *shit*.

A date what I'd refer to as an "Ack-gaffem" or ACGAFM – Another Cunt Gets a Free Meal. She'll allow you to fall into this vortex every time if you like. Especially in the occasional instance where she has a venue in mind from the start. You should deflect this inclination on her part – not so much out of some contrived requirement that you lead the way in *every* goddamn decision, but out of the basic need to keep the deal as convenient and least costly for *you*. If she straight-off has a venue in mind, I say just go with it, providing it's not some swanky-ass bullshit. Then you need to suggest something else, and if she gets indignant, delete her number.

I wish I could tell you that such a stunt might create such a value-spike in her evaluation of you, so as to cause her to suddenly see you as some take-charge Alpha and then compliantly jump into your lap. Just delete the number. You won't hear from her again. She has too many options. Go work on one of what outta be a group of other numbers in your phone.

I'm not gonna talk at great length as to how you should compose yourself on the actual date. Authors like Roosh, Corey Wayne, and Caleb Jones really nail all of this, but if I could be so honored as to be included alongside such in your roster of mentors, the contribution I will add to the consideration of the date itself would be to always be cognizant of the 3 Pillars. Humble yourself before them and abide by them, for they will undoubtedly become part of the core of your own success.

Just met a girl who's the very best yet? With the

biggest tits, the widest hips, and the finest smile? You connect intellectually, philosophically, and share unique interests? Hey, great. But what happens if, for whatever reason, she vanishes after that magical one and only hour? You find someone else just like her, that's what you do, 'cause that other one's gone. If you've managed to uncover a certain "type" that you really fancy, then start the fuck over and find another of that type. Once a girl is "over" you, even if Jesus Christ, Bhudda, Moses, Mohammed, and George fuckin' Washington were to snag her into an intervention as to how she should give such a great guy another shot . . . the core of the matter is how she'll all ready be fucking someone else that she likes even better. Fortunately, *she's replaceable*.

During the course of a date, build a mental picture of the "escalation template" to use toward advancing the physical intimacy, *gradually*, through a sequence of subtle steps of your devising. Please, *please* don't be overly concerned with "going too far" and wrecking the prospect by scaring her off. Although this is absolutely possible, the likelihood pales in comparison to the far greater hazard of taking it too light and having her quizzically think you're a pans, or worse yet, merely the latest candidate for her social media fan-club. Max that interaction.

A key aspect of the Romantic Dark Age that we need to acknowledge is that women are being constantly bombarded by encouragement, as well as incentive to exploit their sexual license and liberties to a scope unprecedented in the history of the Universe.

Not only for the hedonistic thrill, but also, most assuredly for the transactional potential for bettering her situation, especially in an uncertain economic climate, will a woman so readily give up the puss . . . for the right man at the right time.

With the proper experience and practice, coupled with a dash of luck, you'll be the one to join in on all of this. Otherwise, you can still hang back and learn. You'll have dates where, drink in hand, you'll be regaled with tales of her past exploits that'd make Caligula's orgies look like a prudish book club.

It will be an *immense* vexation when a girl hands you all of that shit, and it's epitomized with how *you're* not to get any funny ideas, as she could never like you in "that way".

Barring a structured, committed relationship of some kind . . . it just doesn't mean anything to her. Allow me to make that distinction. The 3rd Pillar refers to the confines of the "connection" you think you've made with a chick you've just met.

Noteworthy Phenomena

We'll have a bit of fun here by listing a few of the more recurrent issues I've run into in my own dating experience thus far. By no means is this an exhaustive list of crap that you could encounter, but an interesting spread of themes that had ultimately become all too familiar to me.

Returning to discussing messaging/phone game and the like, I would definitely caution you against talking to a woman over the phone for more than twenty minutes before you've met. Really, do *not* do this. I can recall barely *any* instances where, after either one, or a sequencing prelude of lengthy phone calls culminated in a date. The best I can do here is theorize that if you talk with her on the phone for a great length – perhaps out of your erroneous notion that you'll "stand out" – she'll find this call to be sufficient enough of an equivalent to a proper date, and simply move on. And I'll add right now, realize that a one-shot deal may have all ready been what she decided on in the *first* place. It's also possible that in the midst of a sizable phone call, either you'll inadvertently say something she finds objectionable, or for whatever reason disqualifies you and bails on what would have otherwise at least been an actual date.

Seriously, *don't* do a call for more than ten minutes or so. Just get a feel for each other's voices and vibe, plan the date and that's it. Test this out for yourself, and do a marathon chat with her – you won't meet.

The previously listed reminds me of a closely related occurrence worthy of mention, and this one is among many that are exclusive to the online dimension . . . chicks that *require* a phone call before meeting. In my area, being Los Angeles & Orange counties, I get this shit primarily from Jews, Armenians, and maybe some other middle-eastern groups. Y'know, they're such entitled princesses, they've got to "interview" you in order to run your ass through their gauntlet of regal prerequisites. Bottom line, you won't meet her. Just delete the message.

The "warm-up" factor. Quite often recently, I've been running into this shit. You meet a chick from an app, and you learn from her that she *just* signed onto this crap for the first time, or is just starting a new tour on there, and you're her first date out of what you can presume will be an endless assortment.

Yeah, I'm liable to charm this chick so masterly as to convince her to log off of the six-month tour she just paid for, so that she can be enraptured in the dazzlingly romantic life we're at the commencement of building together. Don't get too comfortable with that chick – she's gonna be real gone real fast, as there're a multitude of flavors waiting to be sampled. It's like I'm merely the fucking gatekeeper, offering her a warm beckoning into the current dating universe.

"Currently separated" seems to be all the rage on the apps recently. Amazing, how these chicks can't wait to get out there and start fucking around, before the divorce is even drawn up. Consequently, I'm more requently running into this type of situation, where the guy who's either on his way out, or is officially divorced from the woman is still to some degree involved in her dealings. The "Invested Ex", the fuckin' guy is either still paying for some of her shit, or still fucking her or otherwise buzzin' around her 'cause he can't get over it. So you, as the new bro, can expect to either become entangled in some sort of cuck shit, or really, anticipate a very brief romp with that particular chick, as something like that is a big ol' bunch a'problems you don't need.

One particularly memorable illustration of these lessons in recent recollection appears in the form of this Russian chick, currently separated (snort), 32, whose digits I briskly snagged from off of an app. She had kind of a Sissy Spacek look, but perhaps a bit more gaunt. She claimed to be occupied as some kind of property management leasing consultant, supplemented with Uber driving.

Perhaps a day or two after first texting, I was able to coax her into deviating from her afternoon's taxiing itinerary and come to my place. That very hour, she'd mentioned that she was on her way to the car wash, so I suggested she come here for that, as I had a power washer. She rather enthusiastically obliged, and zipped on over.

I then hastily assembled the washing gear, pleased with my little ruse. She rolls up and I direct her to park in a bit of yard space adjacent to the house. She proves to be a rather cute lil' number, true to her pix. *Nothing* astounding, really. You guessed it – a Solid 6. Ooo, whoa.

Donned in a sport blouse and yoga pants, with a flannel overshirt wrapped around her waist, I could indeed determine that she was thin and lean, although I'd yet to be able to spy out the shape of her ass and hips.

We started right off with power washing her slick little Uber ride, taking turns in spraying not only her car, but the two of mine I had parked right there as well.

At various intervals, as rapport was being built, I'd take her gently by the waist, while we circled around the cars. Her body had a supple, yet soft feel to it, and I was pleased.

After a sufficient wash, she seemed about ready to take off, but I was able to capitalize on her indecisiveness by persuading her to come inside and sit down. On this occasion, I happened to not have any booze, and surely, this is a point where the "players" would hammer me over the head with the "you're an idiot if you don't have alcohol" shit, but even if I had, it's doubtful I'd have opted to ply her with such, given the night's worth of Ubering ahead of her.

Anyway, we take seats opposite each other, and I make a concerted effort to hang back, planning to slowly ratchet up the escalation template. She told me about how she was, literally, in between the latest instances of court appearances for her divorce, from whom she made out to be quite the psychotic, emotional, tough-guy, bad-boy asshole muscleman.

"He hates me. He beat me up. So strong, lifts 150lb. weights. I was worried I'd become pregnant if I stayed with him", she ruefully confessed, in a distinct Russian accent. I listened to all of this, receptively, but quite nonplussed. Her two jobs – somehow – worked to combat the $2,200 a month rent for her condo, in addition to whatever other opulence she had going on.

I'd periodically caress her hand, or run a finger over her knee. Soon, the discussion took a more philosophical turn, where she asked me something along the lines of, "What makes you happy?" Taking this as a good enough cue as any, I then stood up over her to reach in for the kiss. She expertly predicted this, snaking her tongue out in anticipation, before my mouth was even close to hers. Following a dramatic make-out as I stood over her still-seated form, I gingerly replied, "*That* makes me happy."

From right then on, more kissing ensued, followed by my attempt at intersplicing this with taking off her blouse. With perhaps a pause of trepidation, she permitted me to sling off her top and unclasp her bra. I'd done this one-handed before, but on this occasion it was all fumbles, as she was even prompted to offer some help. When I did manage to wrangle it off, I was dismayed to find that she had *no* breasts at all. Amazing, the range of variation that exists for this part of the body – some chicks being completely devoid of material up top, while others have a pair of gargantuan, hanging bags.

Still, I proceeded to kiss what little that was there, but after only a moment of this, she felt hastened to cover herself, slinging her bra and blouse back on. Oh well, moving along, I figured it was then time to remove her yoga pants – more like "rip them off" would be a more apt recollection. My first attempt at tugging at her waistband, while she was still seated, was halted smartly, as she made some remark to the effect that she knew "where this would be going", and indicated for me to ease up. I complied, relenting to continue to reside in the "kissing stage", which endured for several more sessions.

After a bit of time, she seemed to incline toward leaving, so she could continue her driving route, but I did detect a certain air of reluctance then, so I opted to exploit this to the best of my perception.

Trapping her in the corner of the room, right by the front door, yet another embrace of kissing ensued. In the midst of this, I made another tug at her waistband, fondling past the wrapped-around flannel. With no more than a second's elapsing, her pants found themselves yanked down to her sneakers, revealing alabaster thighs, snugly draped in a skimpy thong. This too, I tried to slide down, but she halted me abruptly, though not before I'd pulled it to her knees. She off-handedly remarked as to how her vulva was freshly shorn, as she hastily fit her underwear back in place.

Still, in the corner there, we must've gone through a loop-de-loop of at least five rounds of this push/pull sequence, where we'd passionately kiss, as I groped her bare ass and thighs, followed by her pulling her pants back up, and being apparently ready to leave – and then I'd re-launch the process by kneeling down, spinning her around, tossing aside that damn flannel, and yank her pants down again. Her ass was a model of curvaceous, toned splendor.

After a tirade of kissing and touching her ass, I'd spring back up, and spin her back around to face me so we could make-out again. The door was half open, as she was fixating on leaving after each interval of all this, so it was really somethin' when in one instance, she actually kicked the door back shut in a move of submission to the passion of the affair. And "affair" it certainly was – she was still fucking married, look at this shit.

I just couldn't get enough of that ass, but I did finally reach a point of acceptable satiation, tempered by her repeated "attempts" at leaving, so then, surely, I swing the door open and gingerly walked her out. Once in her car, I guided her as she drove back out of the narrow parking spot. She excitedly told me, "We'll talk on the phone tonight." Assured I had maxed the interaction, I contentedly bade her a good night.

I'd now like to see a show of hands from the class as to who thinks I heard from this chick *ever* again. Ah, I do, regrettably, see a few of you motioning to the affirmative. Guess again.

This *recent* example so starkly illustrated not only the principles and phenomena that make for the theme of this book, but also how still, I myself continue to practice poor Game. You see, I must shamefully admit that, after she left, I not only texted to beckon her to just come back later and stay the night, but more atrociously so, I musta messaged/called several more times over the ensuing few weeks. Imagine how that unabated stack of texts looked on her chatlog. Pathetic.

Upon this disclosure, I'll brace myself for the various lambasting from fellas insisting I had "blown it", either through the repeated middling efforts to "revive" the lead, or even for being unable to secure the bang.

Sure, had I been more optimal in my execution, she would have otherwise come scampering back to continue to elaborate on what would be a fulfilling and idealistic romance, in all conventional seriousness . . . and enduring the dubious distinction of having to deal with the emoting, tough-guy semi-ex, who you know would *never* be fully out of the picture.

The "meet & greet". Here's a term that I've run into a bare few times, but as such, make for a stark lil' point worth mentioning. If, while in the preliminary process of planning a date, she refers to this tentative first encounter as a "meet-up", or "meet & greet", excuse yourself from the chat, and delete the message.

Again, I've run into this just enough times as to warrant a pattern, but I'm quite confident that this terminology usage is the calling-card of a certain kind of time-waster. Not only will she get incredibly pissed off and offended if you try to parry this by calling it a "date", the resulting encounter, if it even happens, will be guaranteed to be devoid of physical intimacy.

Another especially shitty element that you may very well experience in dating is when the girl gives you any kind of "advice" on goddamn dating, or even more specifically, starts referencing supposed ways how you can go out there and meet other chicks.

Essentially, trying to "un-sell" herself to you as any kind of viable prospect. God, I hate this shit. When you encounter this, *know* you've officially been written off, so abruptly end the date, as no more time need be wasted.

Though I strongly advocate tapping into a woman's potential for spontaneity by being ready to jump up and go meet her that same hour you first communicated, I'll toss in a quick caution that, if it happens to be around 8 or 9pm or later when you first talk, you might want to delay pitching the date until the next day.

I've run into a few instances where she got all miffed at the proposition of a late night meeting, denouncing it as a "booty-call". Uh yeah, so I guess she can rationalize it in some otherwise constructive manner if you fuck her within forty minutes of meeting her, providing it was midday or something.

A strategy that I've been experimenting with recently is to suggest picking her up at her place to start things off. I don't endorse making this into a standard practice to implement, but every once in a while you'll just feel especially adventurous, or decipher some other factor that suggests coming to get her will help ensure that you meet. Remember, make it as easy as possible for her.

More likely than not, this gesture will merely invoke a mildly defensive response from her, or she'll just deem it as unnecessary, but still be thankful for your "courtesy". However, a distantly possible result could be you showing up to be promptly welcomed into the cozily private setting of her home, where y'all will be free to enjoy some real quality time. So far, I've pulled this off twice.

If I were to imagine, like, a hypothetical *"Open Letter to the Ladies"*, primarily regarding their conduct online, the header of that bastard would be to respectfully request that, if you're not interested, *please* don't respond. Just don't respond. Seems like it's high time somebody finally got chicks wise to the fact that this online shit is *not* a mirror image of itself across the gender line. It is a reverse-imaged universe, by where a man can send out fifty messages and get no replies, while a woman can just *sit there*, send no messages, and *receive* fifty inquiries.

Boy, does it suck ass for a dude when, out of his total quota, the one reply that comes through reads with "not interested, good luck in your search". Each chick on there gets to be a pseudo-celebrity, receiving piles of fan mail, of which she can single out a select few to magnanimously respond to with dubiously artificial well-wishes.

And how about the shit on these profiles, eh? I'll forego analyzing the laundry-lists of meticulously stockpiled requirements a prospective suitor would need to fulfill in order to qualify for the basking in the presence of this snowflake royalty. No, instead, I'll take sec to just shred up the kinds of awful pix so often thrown up on these dealies.

All ready having made reference to the practice of *both* men and women misrepresenting their age and physical stature online, as well as having slammed guys for their habitual laziness in not doing the work of providing pro photos, let me take a few more swings at the gals over some naggingly lame shit that they simply keep on doing in the digital realm.

How about those pix in her profile, where she's either with her kids (gak!), or even better, with a crowd of ten people, and *everyone* else's faces is either crudely scribbled out, or some emoji shit is pasted all over the deal. Really, just use pix with only your damn self in 'em . . . and *only* that. No guy on Earth wants to see shots of your pets, your lunch, various witticisms or inspirational quotes, or that same roster of obligatory travel destinations that every other chick on these apps posts, as part of a truly delusional attempt to beam out as unique.

Maybe I should speak for myself on this last one, but I'll take a wild guess that a given dude has no interest in seeing a girl engage in conventionally masculine activities, such as hitting the shooting range, skydiving, snorkeling, or sporting a team jersey in the crowd of some ball game.

I'm not certain as to if my growing disdain for this trend is primarily grounded in my disinterest in a girl who can be "one of the guys", but perhaps more so in the fact that this shit has gotten so damned monotonous. *Every* chick puts this same shit on her profile. All the more reason to not bother with going past that cover pic, really. Fuck it.

Finally, in this section of oddities and issues, I'll talk a little bit about what may be the single greatest offense a guy can willingly offer upon himself – which is enduring the friend-zone or otherwise let himself be "fan-clubbed" into a chick's ever-growing army of admirers.

In blatantly echoing the stance of the most prominent authors of this material, I'd adamantly urge you, really, to damn near *plead* with you to never entertain such a status with a woman, ever. Like how it is with getting a fancy government job, once you're in, you're in. Once a girl formally relegates you to this platonic status, know that she's disqualified you as a potential romantic partner *permanently*. You'll maintain this regard with her for as long as you're foolish enough to endeavor upon it. Christ, just forget you ever knew her.

I should say now that, in many cases where her classification of you in this less than optimal category will be due to some malfeasance on your part – or what I refer to as "falling below the line" with her, by where you've said or done somethin' that lowers her perception of your value down past a critical threshold.

However, there'll be yet other situations where she just doesn't dig you in "that way", or you're not her type, whatever, and at no real fault of your own.

Regardless of the underlying initiator, know that the end result is the same – the acquisition of *that* woman's intimacy shall remain unattainable indefinitely.

Even if you meet her after a decade's impasse, your "new game" ready in hand to try to implement on her . . . that ultimately negative impression she had of you will surely stand true.

In all though, I really wouldn't worry about this kind of shit coming up, as you'll most likely just never hear from her again. Only maybe two or three times, amazingly, has a girl I dated made a serious go at shelving me into this friend-zone bullshit – and only the first instance of which (ugh) did I stupidly run with it, for not knowing any better.

In today's Romantic Dark Age, between a chick's social media and dating app profiles etc., along with her current bullpen of speed-dial dick, she'll almost certainly have no nagging inclination to recruit you into her conglomerate of validating cheerleaders, so you can keep your pom-poms in storage.

Critique of Apps

The reader may very well find useful a "review" section on some of the front-running dating sites. I'll highlight what pitifully few apps may be worth giving a go, and which to not bother with entirely. Unfortunately, providing this kind of assessment has considerable potential of becoming quickly dated, as a given app can spontaneously alter its policies and programming in such a manner as to either amplify its value or entirely nullify it. Still, the core machinery of what makes this shit what it is will surely stay the same for as long as the technology proliferates.

Match. This "pioneer" of online dating remains the standardized bulwark for those adventurous enough to delve into the digitized dimension. I lovingly term Match as the "least shitty" of all the apps I've used. To refer to *any* of these platforms in an outwardly positive regard always invokes sharp hesitation on my part. As I said earlier, even with as mainstream as it has become, that latent stigmatization endures, by where the user bears this low-level mental nag that some fault or folly on one's part has brought one to this.

Look, just try to set that aside, and utilize the resource. If it brings decent leads, and at even a semi-regular rate, then let's just run with it. Regrettably, online is where I get the vast majority of my leads, and that may very well be the case for you too, so let me show you where you're gonna sign on and where you're not.

As coach Bill Starr stated in his highly sought after text, "The Strongest Shall Survive: Strength Training for Football", if his training program allowed for only one exercise to use, the Power Clean would be it – so, if I had to run with only one dating app, it'd be fuckin' Match.

One of the main reasons for this is the simple fact that, given its historical notoriety and familiarity, there's a sizable population on there. Women *default* to using Match. As a paid app, you can have some semblance of expectation that a few chicks on there might actually want to leave the house for a date.

The platform is based on dynamic browsing, according to set criteria. You can delete the profiles you've either all ready messaged or don't like with relative ease (thought still not in one click, as it should be), and the overall filtration process and interface is functional and has value.

Let me remind you that the substance of these reviews flows within the confines of not only the time period of this writing, but also the geographic location which I operate in, so allow for some potential for variation.

So, given that factor, I will point out that for as long as I've used Match, a couple of *huge* flaws persist. One being that there's no notation of any kind that tells you if someone's profile is actually a fuckin' paid subscriber, or just some damn looky-loo. See, you can browse for free, so who the fuck knows how many of your messages were wasted on chicks who haven't even subscribed. I've seen a couple of other apps utilize a simple remedy to this, by appending a "$" icon or some shit on such profiles, but despite Match's founding-father status, they haven't figured this one out yet.

That leads me to another chief flaw I want to point out. There's a daily "message cap" of around sixty. Now, that might sound like an ample stretch, but remember, of the amount sent out in a day, you could expect to get between zero and two replies. Also, the stupid app is so badly programmed, it won't *tell you* when you've capped out. It just keeps displaying "message sent" prompts. It's only if you check your outbox will you see that your quota stopped. Nice. Also note how this is a male-exclusive leash, with no female equivalent, like say, a daily cap on the inbox. On top of all that, I figure that if I'm *paying* for this shit, I should be able to send out as many messages as I damn well please, when I please.

Fortunately, though, Match offers one-month tours, so grab that shit, max the daily cap, and follow the rules. A final note on that damn cap, as you progressively burn through the population, it'll cease to be an issue, as your quotas will stagger downward throughout the tour.

OkCupid. Among the most stigmatized of the apps, we have OkCupid. Being a fee app, you can fully engage this junkyard without throwin' down a dollar – unless of course, you're fuckin' stupid enough to pay to actually pile your message onto a chick's all ready maxed-out inbox (quite common on there), or worse still, sign up for the "A-list features" and all that crap.

Rock-bottom line as to why OkCupid's paid features

are worthless is that they do *nothing* to filter out any of the garbage. You'll *still* have no way of knowing which profiles are dead, or bots, or scammers – of which proliferate extensively on OkCupid. And transsexuals. Lots of them, and no filter in the search criteria for that either. One of the biggest problems with online dating at large is the absolute lack of any functional regulation, and I don't mean the entirely male-tailored microscopes the administrator Nazis'll have shoved up your ass online, but the complete absence, apparently, of any filtration process in place to stomp out women's profiles that are obviously fake, incomplete, inactive and all that bullshit. Nah, the programmers are apparently only so occupied with implementing preventative measures to ensure that the poor women on there aren't being harassed.

"Anti-chode" functions, such as a chick's profile blanking out once you've messaged her once, or being able to progress with a chat only once she's reciprocated by "matching" you. Cute features, and I do acknowledge the sensibility of their utility, but know that all this kind of shit is tailored for the benefit of *women,* not you. I've yet to see a single one of these apps structured for ease of use for the gentleman. Not one.

As a dude, the main problem you'll have with OkCupid – besides the overall terrible quality of talent – is that there's simply too much noise to contend with, as how it's a free platform, *every* guy on Earth is on there, runnin' his fuckin' bullshit game. While a chick on a paid app can expect to get some huge amount of messages a day, multiply that by some horrifying magnitude, and you'll get the inbox of her free app. I can't believe I ever met anyone off of OKC.

That notion leads me to mention the concurrent

elements that finally caused me to quit using this app. Upon looking over my dating spreadsheet (yeah, I've got one), I found that the overall quality of leads of OKC was just too low, and they took even more effort (messages sent vs. response ratio) to achieve. Ultimately, though, let me tell you what gave me the final push to delete the profile. It got to the point where, when I'd see that little (1) in my inbox, and find that it was a message from OKC, as opposed to Match, I'd feel a nagging dismay, because it'd be practically guaranteed to be total bullshit.

eHarmony. Here's another one I'm sure you've heard is some kind of great shit. Well, it's not. It's just shit. In fact, it's robbery. Don't use it. One, the vehicle for which the browsing is powered is inherently flawed. Upon signing up, the user is prompted to endure a cumbersome questionnaire, directly reminiscent of those goddamn dealies you fill out as part of applying for a retail job, so that, through eHarmony's "algorithm" idiocy, you'll be granted browsing rights *only* to those profiles to be pre-determined as supposedly compatible with your preferences, etc. So, who the hell knows what profiles you might've liked, or how many of 'em there are that you'll never see. I remember the first of only twice that I tried this shit, where I'd be allotted a tiny snippet of matches, scattered amongst a fifty-mile radius. Given the rigmarole required to cancel, I ended up having to actually call my credit card company and just claim it as a fraudulent charge.

A few years later, I figured on trying it once more to see if it had changed, and this time they offered a three-day free trial. Recently, eHarmony phased out the one-month touring option, which would've made it barely palatable, in favor of a six-month minimum. Yeah, either a 6, a 12, or a

24-month option! Holy shit, imagine pinballing around that heap for two years?!

I launched as big a quota as I could in that three days (even got some leads), and then was able to fuckin' cancel. If a paid app doesn't offer *short* term memberships, *don't* use it.

Plenty of Fish. With "fish" in the name, you know somethin's up. Don't use POF. It's garbage. By signing on at all, you're committing an act of self-deprecation, but if you use the paid features on top of that, you should swing from the gallows.

Clearly, the administrators of this site are infinitely more concerned with Gestapo-policing what you message, how much you message, and even if you're cut-paste messaging, than regulating the *titanic* multitude of scammers, bots, camwhores and trannies that populate this ocean of filth.

This is the one and only app I can think of that actually has far more fake profiles than not, and they're surprisingly convincing, with profiles made up of a spread of pix from some average-looking chick, and the whole layout just looks authentic, and so, you'll pick up the digits, and once you send the text, you get sucked into some scam. To this day, I still get the occasional cryptic text from one of those stupid POF scammers that originated from a tour on there from more than a year ago. *Don't* use this app.

Swipe Apps. I don't specialize in "swipe apps", given how I've never gotten any results from them. I've heard that this can vary geographically, but it seems that the core of the issues you'd likely have on 'em is the same as such you'd encounter on any other free app – there's too much noise to contend with, and so, unless you're a model or celebrity, you'll never cut through all the shit.

It's a real shame with these swipe apps, specifically as they appear to be the only corner of the online dating realm where the true, full spectrum of girls can be found, so they present a real enticement. Plus, these apps kinda "get it", squarely placing the browsing emphasis on ease and expediency, given how the whole interface is all about just "swiping" one way or another in as rapid a succession as you can manage.

Give 'em a spin if ya want. Maybe your experience on them will differ from mine, but I'm inclined to recommend that you treat them like any other free app and not bother.

Niche Apps. What I refer to as "niche apps" are either apps like JDate, Inner Circle, The League, that cater to a special population, or whatever other such new and "up & coming" apps that are currently around.

The one issue to consider with these platforms is that, by their very nature of being either new or tailored to a specific audience . . . the population to browse through is simply too small.

Here's what'll happen when you sign onto a niche app – for a one-month tour of upwards of $60, you'll tear through every chick on there in the first hour, leaving twenty-nine days and twenty-three hours of cricket-chirps and tumbleweeds.

You'll know it's time to get offline for a while when you reach the point where you're just getting turned off to the whole idea of meeting women. Enduring too many shitty dates (or not getting any at all) will just get to be too much of a grind. You'll show up at a crowded venue to find that 85% of the other chicks there look way better than her and you figure that if this is the best you can get, then it's not worth it.

You tend to think that these "online girls" are from another planet, as opposed to the ones who see "on the street". The ones you really want. Look, online, they're just more women. Although *it is* true that online you'll find all of the worst and none of the best, there's plenty of crap on the street too – you're just not noticing it. Online, you're making a concerted effort to scrutinize this sliver of "single" women. Conversely, given the whole breadth of concession that men (exclusively) make on their standards, you *can* find chicks online that you'll genuinely evaluate as "good enough".

With that in mind, I'll allot you a final caution regarding online dating. It helps to think of it as a sort of "matrix". Forgive the predictable metaphor, but such a term is simply what first springs to mind. Once a chick gets sucked into this online matrix, she's there to stay. The addiction of infinite flavors to sample, and the indigenous buffet of attention are not to be given up without some extraordinary vigor. Know that the girl you meet from off of there, you're merely borrowing her from the matrix. In the vast majority of cases, after an hour, she'll be over you, and before you even get back to your car, she'll have hopped right back online. And you'll log back on to find her profile is indeed active again, and maybe she'll still be on there next year and the year after that (using the same pix, and shearing a few more years off of her stated age) . . . and on multiple apps, as I've uncovered an absolutely *tremendous* preponderance of "overlap", by where not only the same chicks appear on these things year after year, but spread across several platforms simultaneously. I once met a girl I'd ultimately see posted amongst *eight* different apps. That's gotta be *thousands* of readily available suitors, and yet no one was good enough.

Let this stand as a prompt for you to be doing more of what you should otherwise be engaged in . . . approaching.

Approaching

I remember back, say, around 2013, when I first started to really roll in the Game, you could go on YouTube and see this platoon of various "coaches" scurrying around town, chatting up chicks, predominantly during the day. So-called infield videos of these fellas at work, practicing "daygame", or the process of approaching girls in the midst of their usual daytime business.

In contrast to "nightgame", which would typically take place in the club/bar scene, approaching chicks during the day was presented to the audience as of it were this new sociological breakthrough. "Oh wow, I don't have to go to the clubs anymore. I can go up to chicks during the day". Ostensibly, during the day, some untapped market was put forth by where using systematic frameworks of interaction, you could be assured a receptive female participant base.

Log onto YouTube today, and do a search for "daygame infield videos", and you'll find that, although the level of prevalence it once had hasn't since really tapered down appreciably, the most noticeable change is how it's become common to see MGTOW (Men Going Their Own Way), Black Pill, and "incel" material mingled into the search results, spoofing these infield videos as a joke, lampooning those once mighty daygamers cruising sites such as London, Prague, or Odessa as oafish dreamers, endlessly circling their local town squares, gearing up for their 200 "warm-up" approaches.

That's not to say that, as a single dude, the idea of implementing approaching girls you like as a regular part of your routine is a bad thing. The daygame trend was founded upon a fundamental truth that having the ability to just walk up to a chick and start some kind of conversation is among the most healthful and constructive practices a man can do. Another major component of that factual rationale that spawned daygame is how 95+% of guys just plain can't do it, thus, theoretically at least, freeing up an accessible market for dating prospects.

Well . . . not quite. The area of rationale underlying daygame that's proven to be flawed is the assertion that women would be that dazzled to find some ordinary dude sporting extraordinary boldness in approaching her, fueled by some pre-packaged template of dialogue and mannerisms that'll ideally culminate in either a "number-close", "kiss-close", or the princely achievement of an "insta-date" or "same-day bang".

And the business of this orchestrating the scope of how the intent of your approach is to be played out, according to a spectrum ranging from a passive "indirect", where you make it like you're asking for directions, or making an innocuous comment about an item she's carrying or some shit, and over to the fully "direct" end of the line, where you practically dash up to her, proclaim how you she just caught your eye and she's so cute and all that, and how you'd like to meet her for a date. Direct, indirect, direct, indirect, indirect/direct. Shit! Just go up to her and fuckin' say somethin'.

It'd be pretty hilarious in the clips, when the guy's

play reaches its apparent pinnacle, when he gets out his phone, and *wow*, he gets the number! Or even does a make-out with this chick he just met ten minutes ago . . . neat! No real follow-up, though, as to if anything from that pile of rigorously sought after "connections" ever amount to anything.

Watching this shit on these videos, it's easy to get charged up over it, and that's a fine thing. I'll even include a few resources in the reference section so you can read in-depth as to how to try out some of these methodologies for yourself. And they *do* work.

As it turns out, though, the greater issue is that of prevalence. Prevalence of reliable results, that is. I'll take a wild guess that the idea of spending several hours every week to strut about every outdoor setting you can think of, amassing nine million approaches, the overwhelming majority of which you'll either be brazenly ignored or rattle around in a morose, dead-end chat doesn't strike you as a worthwhile pursuit.

Besides the obvious time-sink a serious approaching regimen is liable to turn into, the biggest issue I've found with the daygame scene is that girls' receptiveness to it is just too low. Between her social media fan-club, dating app leads, and certainly the regular guy(s) she's all ready fucking, one more random dude with the clump to stroll up and talk to her just isn't gonna yield the same "zazz" it once did.

Throughout 2013 to 2015 I had amassed over 600 approaches, and lemme tell ya, without a whole hell of a lot to show for it. Now, looking back, I know that a major part of that lack of results was due to very badly calibrated game on my part. I was *so* fixated on honing the "approach" stage of the interaction that I devoted a pitifully minimal amount of effort into practicing toward advancing those interactions (and all those acquired numbers) into actual dates. If I were to start all that over today, I'm quite confident I'd get more dates. But it would still be an enormously uphill effort of questionable merit.

It's also very important to note that during that time period I was not only working at a Macy's in a major mall, I was also attending university, so it was *so* in my face all the time, a daygaming training ground was an ideal pursuit to mix into the environment I was gonna be enmeshed in either way.

The possibility that your current situation could be like that is what does garner my endorsement to putting in some serious time to make plays – especially if you're a much younger guy, it's really obligatory. However, if, for example, you're not going to any college, and otherwise working full-time, the notion of embarking upon all this day (or night) gaming shit is admittedly pretty unrealistic, even ridiculous.

On top of all that crap, it'd be fuckin' hilarious in its absurdity if it weren't so infuriating, when you do finally get your ass to hit the streets to make plays, and these chicks just give you this look, as if you ruined, like, her whole *year* by approaching her, since you just simply had the misfortune of being a dude she doesn't like the look of, seein' as how they *hate* it when those guys have the audacity to make a move on 'em. Well, ya know what? Tough shit. It's just so . . . in . . . your . . . *face*. The manner in which these chicks parade their asses around today, it's a clap-board sign in glowing neon that reads, "Make Your Play", and so, I'm compelled by a duty to act. If I'm not the stud she's really hoping will read that sign, then she'll just have to endure my game, and relegate the ordeal as simply a part of the cost of doing business.

Conversely, I've had some rather flavorfully pleasant exchanges from that minority of approaches that went well, that although didn't culminate into anything enduring, they ended up providing more substance than actual "dates" for which I'd gone through the formal motions of procuring online.

What's more, the sizable hazard of being duped into meeting someone being deceptive with profile pix is entirely absent in the realm of real world approaching. You make your play, and right then and there, you've met. Straight off, you've each gotten a dose of each other's whole vibe, aura, personality and all of that deal. Any possibility of apprehension before a date, due to concern for misrepresentation is simply non-existent.

That "open market" aspect of approaching is what gives the practice its enduring value. Barring any legitimate blockades, (your own fear doesn't count) you're technically free to engage in the full spectrum of women to be found in person, such that transcends the pitifully narrow sliver of the population to be found on apps.

To finalize this section on approaching I'm not going to let you off that easy. Despite this implication that you may very well *never* get a date from cold-approaching in the current age, it's an integral ability for you to have.

Outside the scope of an exclusive and committed relationship, you, as a man, must make it a prerogative to go up and *say something* to a woman you see that you like. As long as some bro ain't all ready there with her, or some other extenuating obstacle, then *please*, just go and get it over with.

Making your play and getting rejected, ignored, or

otherwise having the interaction go nowhere is a *vastly* superior experience to having backed the fuck down. Anytime I see some lil' cutie out and about all by herself in her goddamn gym outfit, and I end up rationalizing my stupid ass out of not bothering to make that play – nothing in the world bothers me more than *that*.

Part Four

Resources

Given the intentionally ancillary nature of this book, I've deemed it proper to include a list of the primary influences I use in shaping my own philosophies and practices pertinent to this subject matter. Not a sprawling list, but just a few sources, really, is all one should need to team up with *Solid 6* as companion pieces.

My materials, as well as those referred to here should be approached in a Bruce Lee/Clarence Bass style of receptiveness, where you take what you've found to work for you, and leave the rest, as these topics tend to be particularly free-flowing and polarizing, contingent upon individual experience.

Roosh V

This gent's work quickly became a major component of influence and inspiration for me. Known so infamously as among the most controversial as well as inflammatory authors in "Manosphere/Red Pill/Game" circles, if not the world at large, Roosh proved to be an undeniably talented writer, volunteering to chronicle and share his vast expanse of unique experience, and to do so in an engagingly witty prose.

Of his published works, *Bang, Day Bang, 30 Bangs, Game*, and *Lady* are not only immensely entertaining, but strikingly informative. *Game* is truly the pristine embodiment of the best he has to offer as a writer and coach.

Unfortunately, in recent times, a sharp bias on my part has arisen in severe criticism of Roosh. In the wake of his dabbling with hallucinogens, and very tragically, in conjunction with suffering the trauma of losing his sister, Roosh underwent a certain "transitional phase", by where practically overnight, he not only embraced Christianity (a well-worn cliché move if there ever was one), but fully denounced his previous stances on casual sex, courtship, dating, and a host of other topics relating to intergender dynamics. Predictably, this reversal was met with a mix of bewilderment and resentment by his staunchest readers, but not without it being fully embraced by a minority cabal of mega ass-kissers.

Further, his forum used to be my #1 go-to resource for not only counsel on dating and approaching issues, but as a database for world news and current affairs. However, upon his transition, he promptly outlawed pretty much any posting of value, banned any member who'd make a stink about it (I stayed out of all this shit, logged off, and stopped using it, thus still retaining my membership), and stripped the forum down to a neutered shell of its former self.

The one important positive to all of this is the fortunate timing of how he wrote *Game* shortly *before* he transformed into this wandering vagabond street-preacher, the likes of which the world all ready has more than enough of.

Although his forum was great in its prime, there were times where I'd get a bit worn, when I'd post questions, and if the slightest inclination was given that I might be fixated on any individual chick for more than five minutes, I'd be hammered by seasoned members as a "ONEitis, blue-pill beta". I'd just get sick of hearing this shit in response to everything.

As it stands presently, Roosh's forum is of immensely limited value, with a scant minority of senior members still adhering, batting back and forth a limited array of topics, and virtually all of the material he personally puts out is garbage that I can't in good conscience endorse. Cookie-cutter Christian-themed tropes and musings, mingled with conspiracy rants of how the origin and maintenance of every conceivable ill of society is the responsibility of a global plotting hosted by Jews, gays, and socialists.

I'd tell you to buy *Game* and stack it on your shelf next to *Solid 6*, but Roosh has since removed the bulk of his books from publication, deeming them to be "sinful".

Rollo Tomassi

Standing shoulder-to-shoulder with (the old) Roosh, or maybe even superseding him, Rollo is the premiere writer on intergender understanding. The real deal, his series of books are as insightful as they are expansive. So far, his *The Rational Male* series is comprised of three volumes. Get them now, read them, and re-read them. I'd say to also give them to other men who are in dire need of this truly unique education, but they're probably not tough enough to deal with the weight of the enlightenment that these books offer.

The one and only zing that I can think of toward Rollo's books is merely the fact that, at least in regard to his first book, there must've been little, if any proof-reading, as it's heavily peppered with grammatical and typographical errors, which not only emanate an inherently displeasing aesthetic, but also ends up sapping the volume's credibility. Hopefully, he intends to go back over the texts in order to re-release a properly polished edition.

Caleb Jones

Yet another one of my favorite authors, and the prime example of my recommended "take what works & leave the rest" evaluation is Caleb Jones, or "BlackDragon" as he's commonly known online.

A uniquely insightful and thought-provoking author, Jones maintains two blogs, where he posts predominantly on topics ranging from economics and politics to relationships, dating, intersexual dynamics and Game.

What makes him stand out is his very untraditional and controversial stance on the idea of monogamous relationships. This stance being definitively adversarial. A hard-lining advocate of assorted polyamorous, open-relationship platforms, Jones fully endorses the idea that people simply never evolved for exclusive pair-bonding geared for an enduring stretch of time.

Now, I'm not too sure as to what extent I agree with all of this, and so, at least presently, here we arrive at such portions that I leave at the table. However, in considering his tenets concerning the importance of attaining economic self-sufficiency and independence, prioritizing your own needs first, and building your best
self toward optimizing your appeal to women – I feel that he does consistently great writing.

Acknowledging the inherent limits of the value of cold-approaching, but still endorsing it as a critically valuable practice, Jones is a big advocate of online dating. Consequently, his is one of the very few publications that puts out consistent – and accurate – articles on how one can both navigate, as well as profit off of that treacherous market. Many of his articles on dating I've actually been able to go out and test, verifying them to be authentic. Now that's quality product. Even then, though, I'll have to admit that I won't be buying either his books or seminars. Looking at the price ranges and somewhat dubious claims of such, I think I can do without. His blogs will suffice just fine.

That point does prompt me to mention a grievous little practice that occurs periodically within Manosphere/Red Pill/Game circles. Virtually every one of these major authors, at one point or another, will get caught up in a "mini-scandal" of sorts, resulting in his close contemporaries diving into the water to converge on him, making a serious effort to discredit his entire platform. Over the span of several days or more, you'll see these dudes runnin' around YouTube and Twitter, givin' each other "Turkish Revenge". It passes though, and stabilizes, but such incidents cause you to re-evaluate the author's credibility. It really does. And in the case with Roosh, where the author does a complete reversal, you're really prompted to question the very validity of his material.

I chose to cite this in my summarization of BlackDragon, as how recently, social commentator and daygame champion Nick Krauser did a post absolutely *slamming* Jones, dismissing him as a cuckold and charlatan. The interesting post did indeed cause me to seriously re-consider my aligning with Jones' work, as I also find Nick Krauser to be a significant influence of mine as well.

Yes, Caleb Jones is a middle-aged dude with a lackluster physique, which he'd freely admit the improvement of such is an ongoing struggle for him, and in a further effort toward maintaining a youthful visage, he's opted to donning a sort of hair-weave toupee that, in some photos, looks like a coonskin cap.

As Krauser glaringly observes, Jones took to raising another man's kid as his own, solicits prostitutes, and otherwise engages in "sugar-daddy game", by where the companionship and affection of optimally attractive women is specifically paid for, and finally, his seminars and club memberships and such are of a ridiculous price range. His claims as to this sprawling expanse of sexual conquests, even with some monetary greasing of the wheels, do strike the reader as dubious and snake-oily.

Krauser makes some apt points, surely. Ultimately, though, I feel inclined to cutting Jones a break. He does some of this shit out of acceptance of the reality of his situation. He's striving to optimize the quality and frequency of his successes as best as his resources allow him in an increasingly slanted, demented, and entirely de-regulated sexual marketplace, where getting a hold of even a genuinely crappy girl is a slaughter.

This doesn't mean that I think you should buy his shit. No, I think Krauser was right on that one. And hell, that goes for the bulk of these various conventions, boot-camps, seminars, and the like that a lot of these guys offer – the costs are insane.

But to entirely dismiss Jones as a credible source would be a mistake, since he has some of the very best articles on both dating and being a better man.

Nick Krauser

As I just asserted, Nick is an especially astute writer. Based in the United Kingdom, he's established himself as, perhaps, the most world-renown authority on daygame. Sporting his own series of highly-priced books, Nick meticulously outlines a blueprint for achieving rapid success with women, chronicling the complete expanse of the seduction process, from the boardwalk to the bedroom.

His books look well-polished and expansive. I've yet to check any of 'em out, but I may yet. Nick is very literate, and in recent times he's tilted a lot of his postings away from daygaming toward discussing the monumental expanse of literature he's engrossed himself in.

Part of this change in emphasis stems from the inclination that a lot of these "career-players" develop upon entering their 40s, that being to "retire" from the pick-up scene, settle down and start families. Well, uh, given how such a prospect is squarely at odds with their heightened state of awareness of not only the ways of the world, but of female nature, I'm not sure as to how feasible that is.

Not without his detractors, Krauser has incurred criticism, not only from the obligatory railings of both indignant women and feminized men, but it should also be noted that he's a committed white-supremacist, in addition to being a rabid anti-Semite, and like Roosh, embraces the proposition that the imminent destruction of the universe is the collective aim of a collaboration among Leftists, Jews, and homosexuals. Again, glean the value, discard the rest.

A few more authors I'd highly recommend . . .

Corey Wayne
Rich Cooper
Donovan Sharpe
Gonzalo Lira
Greg Adams
Shawn T. Smith

Afterward

There will be times when you want to give up. The seemingly endless grind required to assemble leads, and the raw mental fatigue of the first dates to nowhere that they end up as. Always meeting a new girl, again and again, going through those introductory motions, perpetually.

To continually *steel* yourself into as close a state as possible of actually feeling . . . nothing. That next time your mind is truly obligated to be convinced that you've really "got something special" with such-&-such chick, but way deep down at the core, another part of your thought process has been conditioned to emerge, its sole purpose being to combat the former sentiment, poised to help you to brace yourself from that all too likely aftermath of her simply disappearing, or otherwise voicing some apathetic dismissal of that brief episode together. Such that you tried to simply let yourself cherish, free of any regard to what it might lead to. But all too often, there was just not enough time. That pleasant interaction proved to be way too fleeting, and there's nothin' you can do about it.

I know these feelings. After what proves to be the latest first date to nowhere, or even merely the slough itself of even getting that far just wears you down to the point of quitting. You'll have "gone your own way", assured that you've become disavowed from dating permanently. Ya end up thinkin' that nobody's interested and nobody cares. The epic bullshit of it all will leave you to marvel at how couples come together at all in these times.

Right now, I could cast my mind over the countless instances I've endured this mental wrangling. Yeah, I'll know that I'm over and past it all, sure. But then, in time, that chance occasion will come along when, quite inadvertently or otherwise, I'll steal a furtive glance at the goods, and it makes me think of that hit song from *Whitesnake*, "Here I Go Again". That object of my desire will emerge, seemingly out of the very ether, I'll both freeze and melt at the same time, deep inside . . . and the whole process will start anew.

Though I was *sure* of being done with all of this shit, I'll find that such a sentiment runs paradoxically with that "Here I Go Again" moment. Might not be for a good while, but that moment *will* make its familiar appearance time and again.

Perhaps what I'd designate as a final piece of advice for the reader would be that if he has some grandiose plan to marry and build a family, a dynasty or whatever . . . it'd probably be in his most sensible interests to shelve such aspirations, if not ditch them entirely.

It's gotten to the point where to expect a particular chick to stay around for any sizable stretch of time is an aspiration so far-fetched as to be considered asinine. It's so easy for a man to become entrenched in a vortex of hopeless desperation, willing to latch onto any shit deal that he feels will slake his feelings of lacking and emptiness.

I've known far too many men – and the bulk of such being very close to me – end up not only completely restructuring their lives, but also outright reprogramming their very fucking minds in order to conform to what they *believe* will optimally facilitate the flourishing of a relationship . . . and on top of such, with women of unspeakably low quality.

To borrow core rhetoric shared by both Rollo Tomassi and Rich Cooper, you need to become your own "mental point of origin", constructing and maintaining a life based on goals, the success of which are *not* contingent on a specific someone going along with them. In addition to that notion, I'll be god-double-damned before I orchestrate my own life's infrastructure around satisfying anyone else's whims.

I wish that I could fully assure you that you'll not only figure out what you're looking for, but also find it. Some things just aren't the way they were in past generations. The manner in which men and women were brought together, practically in accordance with a societally-conditioned sequence of sorts. I don't think that either our parents, or even many of our direct contemporaries will ever fully comprehend as to how things are now.

While *Solid 6* is not likely to provide for you the foundation on which to build those far-reaching plans that you may still yearn for, I do feel that I can assure you that, as opposed to before you beheld this chronicle, that at least every once in a great while, you'll snag a piece a' puss.